The Christian Peace Shelf

The Christian Peace Shelf is a selection of Herald Press books and pamphlets devoted to the promotion of Christian peace principles and their applications. The editor (appointed by the Mennonite Central Committee Peace Section) and an editorial board from the Brethren in Christ Church, the General Conference Mennonite Church, the Mennonite Brethren Church, and the Mennonite Church, represent the historic concern for peace within these constituencies.

FOR SERIOUS STUDY

Durland, William R. *No King but Caesar?* (1975). A Catholic lawyer looks at Christian violence.

Enz, Jacob J. *The Christian and Warfare* (1972). The roots of pacifism in the Old Testament.

Hershberger, Guy F. *War, Peace, and Nonresistance* (Third Edition, 1969). A classic comprehensive work on nonresistance in faith and history.

Hornus, Jean-Michel. *It Is Not Lawful for Me to Fight* (1980). Early Christian attitudes toward war, violence, and the state.

Kaufman, Donald D. *What Belongs to Caesar?* (1969). Basic arguments against voluntary payment of war taxes.

Lasserre, Jean. *War and the Gospel* (1962). An analysis of Scriptures related to the ethical problem of war.

Lind, Millard C. *Yahweh Is a Warrior* (1980). The theology of warfare in ancient Israel.

Ramseyer, Robert L. *Mission and the Peace Witness* (1979). Implications of the biblical peace testimony for the evangelizing mission of the church.

Trocmé, André. *Jesus and the Nonviolent Revolution* (1975). The social and political relevance of Jesus.

Yoder, John H. *The Original Revolution* (1972). Essays on Christian pacifism.

_____. *Nevertheless* (1971). The varieties and shortcomings of Christian pacifism.

FOR EASY READING

Beachey, Duane. *Faith in a Nuclear Age* (1983). A Christian response to war.

Drescher, John M. *Why I Am a Conscientious Objector* (1982). A personal summary of basic issues for every Christian facing military involvements.

Eller, Vernard. *War and Peace from Genesis to Revelation* (1981). Explores peace as a consistent theme developing throughout the Old and New Testaments.

Kaufman, Donald D. *The Tax Dilemma: Praying for Peace, Paying for War* (1978). Biblical, historical, and practical considerations on the war tax issue.

Kraybill, Donald B. *Facing Nuclear War* (1982). A plea for Christian witness.

_____. *The Upside-Down Kingdom* (1978). A study of the synoptic Gospels on affluence, war-making, status-seeking, and religious exclusivism.

Miller, John W. *The Christian Way* (1969). A guide to the Christian life based on the Sermon on the Mount.

Miller, Melissa, and Phil M. Shenk. *The Path of Most Resistance* (1982). Stories of Mennonite conscientious objectors who did not cooperate with the Vietnam draft.

Sider, Ronald J. *Christ and Violence* (1979). A sweeping reappraisal of the church's teaching on violence.

Steiner, Susan Clemmer. *Joining the Army That Sheds No Blood* (1982). The case for biblical pacifism written for teens.

Wenger, J. C. *The Way of Peace* (1977). A brief treatment on Christ's teachings and the way of peace through the centuries.

FOR CHILDREN

Bauman, Elizabeth Hershberger. *Coals of Fire* (1954). Stories of people who returned good for evil.

Moore, Ruth Nulton. *Peace Treaty* (1977). A historical novel involving the efforts of Moravian missionary Christian Frederick Post to bring peace to the Ohio Valley in 1758.

Smucker, Barbara Claassen. *Henry's Red Sea* (1955). The dramatic escape of 1,000 Russian Mennonites from Berlin following World War II.

WHAT BELONGS TO CAESAR?

A DISCUSSION ON THE CHRISTIAN'S RESPONSE TO PAYMENT OF WAR TAXES

Donald D. Kaufman

A Christian Peace Shelf Selection

HERALD PRESS
Scottdale, Pennsylvania
Kitchener, Ontario

Developed jointly by the Mennonite Church, Scottdale,
Pennsylvania, and the General Conference Mennonite
Church, Newton, Kansas

82 83 84 85 86 87 88 10 9 8 7 6 5 4 3

Dedication

"It is not out of lack of patriotism, but out of true concern for this country and this planet that I protest war taxes."
— Donald R. Klassen
(April 15, 1969)

"I really am a God-fearing American. The World Council of Churches may not mean what it says, but it says that war is contrary to the will of God. The government was asking me to defy God's will by paying it to make war, and I did not have the courage to defy God's will. The government itself said that it trusted in God — though whoever says he trusts in God and carries a gun mightily mistrusts either God or the gun. If it is not treasonable to say so, I am an American who trusts in God."
— Milton Mayer
(September 1, 1962)

"Must the citizen ever for a moment, or in the least degree, resign his conscience to the legislator? Why has every man a conscience, then? I think that we should be men first, and subjects afterward. It is not desirable to cultivate a respect for the law, so much as for the right. . . .
"Under a government which imprisons any unjustly, the true place for a just man is also a prison."
— Henry David Thoreau
(1817-62)

"But Peter and the apostles answered, 'We must obey God rather than men.'"
— *Acts* 5:29 (RSV)

". . . it being our Principle to feed the Hungry and give the Thirsty Drink; — we have dedicated ourselves to serve all Men in every Thing that can be helpful to the Preservation of Men's lives, but we find no Freedom in giving, or doing, or assisting in any Thing by which Men's Lives are destroyed or hurt."
— Excerpt from Mennonite and Dunkard Petition to the Colonial Assembly of Pennsylvania, 1775.

This book is dedicated to the people of our world who have suffered and who continue to suffer at the hands of demonic powers.

The Tribute Money

By Peter Paul Rubens

Preface

It was during my three years (1955-58) at Mennonite Biblical Seminary at that time located in Chicago that I was first alerted to the idea that paying taxes designated for war might be inconsistent with the demands of Christian discipleship. The discovery came about quite unexpectedly as I was reading William Warren Sweet's book, *The Story of Religion in America.*

Ever since then the war tax problem has been a special concern and I have been impressed, not only with the large amount of literature on this subject, but even more with the growing number of persons in this country and abroad who are questioning the propriety of paying taxes that are used largely for war purposes. In recent years there seems to be a growing uneasiness about this problem and a significant number of people are determined to do something about it. To be sure, the variety of responses to this ethical problem is somewhat bewildering. On the one hand, it has been encouraging to see people struggling with the issue because they believe that it is most urgent that we reexamine our doubtful assumptions about what the Bible says on this subject. On the other hand, the feeling expressed by some that "there is no moral responsibility on my part for how the state spends tax money" is disturbing. Is it really true that "we are not responsible for the use of the taxes once Caesar shears us"? I readily admit that the problem of war taxes has no easy solution, but I would hope that there could be a greater measure of agreement in recognizing this as a problem for the Christian.

My purpose is to clarify the war tax issue and to see the alternatives from a Christian point of view. In addition to providing a survey of the history of taxation I have examined a number of interpretations regarding scriptural references which are often used to justify unquestioning obedience to governmental tax demands. One of the biggest hurdles for Christians to overcome in considering the war tax issue is the almost universal assumption that the Bible speaks with one voice regarding the necessity of tax payment to governments by its citizens. This is fully confirmed in the experience of Walton N. Hackman, executive secretary of the Committee on Peace and Social Concerns for the Mennonite General Conference, who was asked to meet with a particular Mennonite congregation which was making a study of the tax situation. On January 12, 1968, he wrote:

> This has been a most helpful experience in seeing the situation at the "grass roots." The greatest difficulty which I have sensed is not in finding an acceptable way of tax refusal, rather it is in the area of education, in the area of the biblical teachings concerning the payment of taxes. Many Mennonites feel that there is an indisputable biblical mandate to pay to Caesar what is Caesar's. The context in which Christ spoke those words is very often not taken into account by those who hold this position.

One might ask: Can the Scriptures provide us with the means of testing whether or not payment of war taxes constitutes a form of idolatry? It is my conviction that a careful and thorough study of the biblical references often used to justify unqualified obedience to governmental demands, even without the correction or balance which other passages provide, leaves room for differing interpretations. I hope that this study helps to make that more evident. Obviously, time did not allow me to examine or digest all the commentaries and articles dealing with the four texts selected. To list the several positions on each passage and their supporting arguments would have taken me far beyond my intentions. Nevertheless, this beginning should suggest the possibilities of interpretation when each passage is seen in the context of the historical situation and the total biblical message.

In section III I have tried to articulate what I considered to be a Christian basis for arriving at a position on the war tax issue. Section IV illustrates how various people have attempted to resolve this ethical issue in their unique historical situations.

Since I recognize both the limitations of this study and the urgent need for it, I strongly urge more individuals and groups within our congregations to investigate and discuss the implications of paying taxes in the light of the total biblical message and in terms of their Christian commitment and discipleship. The bibliographies at the end of this book and in other books should provide ample resource material for fruitful dialogue. This is one excellent way in which congregations can truly become communities of discernment. If we are unconcerned and refuse to investigate issues such as this with open-minded study and Spirit-directed concern, we too are likely to become "a people without discernment" (Isaiah 27:11b).

This study is offered to the reader with the following thought:
"He who takes a stand is often wrong;
He who fails to take a stand is always wrong."

ACKNOWLEDGMENTS

In addition to the writings of numerous individuals included in this book, the following persons have been of great help to the author:

Bennie Bargen, who during my college years probably planted the first seeds of concern which grew eventually into my present awareness of the war tax problem;

William Klassen, who generously referred me to resource persons and materials and who corrected the manuscript for improved readability;

John M. Swomley, Jr., who kindly took valuable time from his schedule to offer suggestions and criticisms of the manuscript;

Howard Charles, who shared a deep concern for the problem as it is found in the New Testament materials and who graciously wrote an excellent introduction for this book;

John Howard Yoder, who helped to motivate me in this discipleship effort by demonstrating what a person could do to witness to government about war taxes;

Walton N. Hackman, who was prompt to recognize the manuscript's potential for publication and who took the initiative in making a wider circulation possible;

Darrell W. Fast, who found the necessary sponsors and who made other publishing arrangements through numerous rounds of committee correspondence;

Ellrose D. Zook, who patiently worked with me in getting the manuscript so that the book would be useful to those who needed it;

Mrs. Evelyn Habegger, who typed the original manuscript under the pressures of a tight schedule;

And finally, my wife, Eleanor, who not only served as a sounding board for ideas, but who shares with me the convictions which grow out of this concern.

Introduction

The Irish poet, William Butler Yeats, once composed an obituary for his close friend John Synge. "He was," wrote Yeats, "a patriotic man who . . . gave his country not what it wanted but what it needed . . . a kind of perpetual last day, a round of trumpets and a summoning up to judgment." In this tribute to his friend Yeats put his finger on a problem that has plagued society from antiquity. The problem may be formulated in various ways, but in essence it is the rights and the duties of the individual *vis-a-vis* the state.

The solutions to this problem have been widely diverse. In the main, three broad approaches are possible: the deification of the state with the total subservience of the individual to it; the anarchical position which regards the state as the expression of the demonic with which no voluntary cooperation is legitimate; and the intermediate stance which assumes limited prerogatives of state authority over the individual and allows for a measure of personal dissent. It is the third of these basic approaches which characterizes the democratic societies of modern times.

Within this broad solution, however, there is much latitude for various formulations of the precise role of the respective entities, the state and the individual. Indeed no permanent normative solution can be worked out since both the individual and the state are not static, but constantly changing elements in the problem. Even the matter of the official interpretation of the law that governs the mutual relationship between the individual and the state is not without its variable elements. The result is the presence of a perennial problem that may express itself from time to time and place to place in a great variety of forms.

One of the particularly difficult areas for Christians who believe that the confession of Jesus as Lord involves a commitment to a way of love is the demand made by the state for support of its military operations. These demands may take different forms depending upon the situation. In general, however, there are the demands for personal services and for economic support. The latter is derived largely through compulsory taxation. In the historic peace church tradition there has been widespread conviction that the first of these two demands is in conflict with Christian discipleship. No comparable conviction either in extent or depth of feeling exists with regard to the latter.

This situation in part is to be explained both by the general assumption that the Bible frowns upon the refusal to pay government tax and the way in which military appropriations have been an accepted part of government spending. Today, however, the situation has somewhat changed. The amounts that the United States government is devoting to military purposes have risen to the point where huge sums are now being spent in this way even in peacetime. The influence of militarism and of the military establishment in our society has become enormous. The news media have underscored this fact. Furthermore, a current surcharge tax has been closely associated in the popular mind with the financing of the Vietnam war. Thus it has come to be regarded as a specific war tax. Indeed, it is considered as a tax for a war which is increasingly regarded as rather remote from the biblical understanding of the proper role of the state, namely, the maintenance of order and peace.

In this context the present study by Donald Kaufman is especially appropriate. He rightly reexamines the biblical basis for the nature and extent of the Christian's responsibility to the state in the area of tax payment and seeks to formulate general theological guidelines for conduct in this relationship. The author does not offer a single pattern of response, but lists various options. Obviously not all Christians will agree in regard to what is their Christian duty in this matter. But no one can give careful attention to this booklet without having the issues clarified and his conscience sharpened. It is to be hoped that this study will be widely read, seriously discussed, and that out of it will come conduct that will consistently embody the gospel of love that we as Christians profess.

Howard H. Charles
Goshen Biblical Seminary

Contents

	Preface	7
	Introduction	11
I.	Historical Survey of Taxation	17
II.	An Examination of Biblical Passages Often Used to Justify an Absolute, Unquestioning Obedience to Governmental Demands	32
III.	Argument Against the Payment of War Taxes	57
IV.	Historical Survey of Nonpayment Positions and Practices	71
V.	Conclusion	86
	Notes	98
	Bibliography	104
	Index	123

I

Historical Survey
of Taxation

Taxation in Ancient Times

Taxation, in the sense of regular imposts levied by authority upon wealth, is a comparatively late development in man's history. Yet the beginnings of this burdensome and trouble-breeding institution are very ancient. In earliest times taxes were paid in goods rather than money. Levies were unnecessary because all wealth was common wealth. With the rise of individualism and fixed residence it was inevitable that certain possessions held as private property by individuals should be set aside for common use.

The history of taxation appears to be the history of civilization. Taxes can be defined as "a compulsory contribution to the support of government, local or federal, civil or ecclesiastical."[1] Terms which designate some form of taxation are the following: "assessment," "forced labor," "tribute," "import duty," "tariff," "toll," "tax," "half-shekel tax," and "enrollment" (for tax purposes).

In the study of taxation in the Bible, two patterns about the practice become obvious: Israel's history of taxation under self-government and her experiences as tributary to successive conquerors.

In the first glimpses of Hebrew history, no such institution as taxation appears. Nomadic communities had no regular system of taxation, nor did they have use for any. Of course, voluntary presents were given by the less powerful to the more powerful in return for protection or other advantages. Apparently Abraham was one who voluntarily gave a tenth "of all" the spoils (Genesis 14:20).

The transition from this primitive custom of giving presents voluntarily to those which were expected and eventually demanded was fatally easy. Genesis 32:13-21; 2 Kings 16:8; 17:4. In Egypt, where the Pharaohs actually owned the state, a heavy tax in kind was exacted of all Egypt during the seven years of plenty. Some 20 percent of all the produce of the land during the prosperous years was kept aside and stored. Egypt was thus spared the worst consequences of her own years of leanness and became a source of supply for other countries during the famine.

The first evidence of what corresponds to compulsory taxation by the Israelites appears when they compelled the previously unconquered Canaanites to do forced labor. Joshua 16:10; 17:13; Judges 1:28-35. This may have set a precedent. Both David and Solomon pressed aliens into slave labor on the construction of the temple. 1 Chronicles 22:2; 2 Chronicles 2. Even the Israelites themselves were compelled to do forced labor in building the temple (1 Kings 5:13) under Solomon. To the Hebrews this act was a mark of despotism. In practice oriental kings were despots who operated on a program of exploitation, slavery, and high taxes. Apparently they could not take one without the other.

In all probability it was Solomon who first introduced state taxes in Israel. During the period of the judges Israel had no army or royal court to support. Later during the reign of Saul, we hear for the first time of a standing army in the history of Israel. 1 Samuel 13:1f. Although no mention is made of royal revenues during Saul's kingship, a half century later Solomon carefully divided his kingdom into twelve districts for purposes of more efficient taxation. 1 Kings 4:7 ff.

We know that Samuel tried to stop the people from choosing a king (1 Samuel 8:10-18) by describing the burdens and evils which this innovation would place upon the common people. He felt that human kingship would result in abject slavery for the people because the king would (1) establish a standing army consisting of draftees and professional warriors; (2) confiscate the people's lands and give those to the servants; (3) impose heavy taxes upon them; and (4) force them to perform *corvee* labor.[2]

King David seems to have been able to maintain an army without taxing the people in money or in kind. Nevertheless, it was the census of the people ordered by David (2 Samuel 24) which was very likely intended

> . . . to furnish a basis for a methodical distribution of the military burdens and taxes; but Solomon was the first monarch to systematize the furnishing of foodstuffs (1 Kings 4:7-28), and to demand toll from the merchants (10:15), and he, moreover, made the lot of the people an inordinately heavy one (12:4), probably imposing an additional money tax. The later kings again received only voluntary gifts from their subjects, as is recorded of the time of Jehoshaphat and Hezekiah (2 Chronicles 17:5; 32:23), a money tax being levied in time of war only, when the demands of victorious enemies had to be satisfied (2 Kings 15:20; 18:35).[3]

This meant that Solomon's court depended partially on its own subjects for support in addition to the tribute or gifts received from subject peoples and foreign governments, as well as on tolls collected from caravans and traders. 1 Kings 4:22 ff.; 10:14-29. Judah's burden of taxes became so heavy that when Rehoboam succeeded his father the people hoped for a lighter "yoke" (1 Kings 12:1 ff.). Instead the people were taxed even more heavily. Jeroboam and others attributed the division of the kingdom to the oppressive taxation and forced labor exacted by Solomon.

The obligation of rendering tribute needs further clarification. Reference has already been made to forced labor as a form of "tribute." J. A. Sanders defines it as, "A compulsory contribution exacted by one prince or state of another, or by a superior power of an inferior, as in a suzerainty treaty."[4] Egyptian, Babylonian, and Assyrian historical texts provide numerous illustrations where exaction of tribute is a recurring boast of the conqueror. These ancient kingdoms regularly imposed tribute upon conquered peoples; it was in fact a standard procedure for the times. In most instances, the tribute was paid by the inferior power in the treaty to the superior. According to Herodotus, the ruling nation paid no taxes. Tax paying was the duty of subjugated peoples.

As long as Israel and Judah were independent political units, their rulers frequently received tribute from foreign princes and peoples. Often these enforced contributions were in the form of precious metals, works of art, commodities, or slaves. Later when the tide of history turned, the Jewish people had to pay tribute to the political powers of the "Fertile Crescent." Sometimes the demands for tribute came from several directions simultaneously. To meet these obligations often meant severe deprivation and more taxes, such as occurred when Pharaoh Neco exacted a gold and silver tribute from King Jehoiakim. 2 Kings 23:35.

Sanders points out that "Tribute is to be distinguished from the booty which the conqueror forcefully takes in war."[5] Tribute was usually the price which a country chose to pay for a measure of military security. Some, if not all, of these alliances proved to be very costly. In case of a rebellion, the indemnity for an unsuccessful uprising was always far heavier than the tribute.

The Persians were largely responsible for beginning a system of taxation which reached into the purses of the common people. As compared to a tribute given to a foreign master by indigenous princes, this system was administered directly in each Persian province by a Persian satrap. Ezra 4:13. Later in Hellenistic times, the office of tax collecting was not assigned by the foreign king to his local representatives, but rather farmed out to the highest bidder, who had the help of the army in collecting the taxes. Eduard König contends that "the repugnance of the free Israelites to the payment of a money tax was overcome by the postexilic foreign rulers. . . . The taxes often grew to be an especially heavy burden under the Ptolemaic and Seleucidan kings."[6] These kings controlled Palestine from approximately 301 BC to 65 BC.

According to Josephus, the Jewish historian, these rulers employed tax-farmers, who, of course, tried not only to collect the taxes required by the rulers, but also to derive a large personal profit in addition. It was the proverbial crookedness and "graft" of these tax collectors or their local agents, which made the system so hateful to the Jews. This practice established by the Ptolemies in fact introduced a principle which prevailed through all subsequent Jewish history and was the cause of much suffering and discontent. Under this system of exacting unfair taxes, men of eminent rank would bid for the taxing privileges or concessions for certain periods of time.

Joseph ben Tobiah and his son Hyrcanus served as tax-gatherers or collectors for more than 20 years and were thereby able to accumulate immense riches. 2 Maccabees 3:1 — 4:6 reports that a large sum of money had been deposited in the temple of Jerusalem by "Hyrcanus, son of Tobias" when Heliodorus was sent to confiscate it in 187 BC. Although Joseph Tobias enjoyed a reputation for leniency with his own people, at times he' would kill people (or have them killed) for refusing to pay their taxes and then confiscate their possessions. [7] Perhaps he learned this procedure from neighboring kings who contrived to lay hands on the estates of the noble families who fell under their displeasure or who failed to pay the heavy taxes.

By and large this system of taxation also prevailed under Roman rule except that the governors or procurators collected the regular taxes, such as the land tax and poll tax, and the direct taxes were not farmed out. However, the customs or tolls levied upon exports and imports were sold to the highest bidders, who were called "publicans." The fact that certain Jewish individuals were helping the Romans in the exaction of the heavy taxes imposed upon the Jews, plus the rapacity of some tax collectors who took advantage of the indefiniteness of the tariffs, made this class of officials hateful to the people. Tax collectors were always under the suspicion of being extortioners and probably they were in most instances. Whatever they were able to raise over the amount of their contract with the government went into their own pockets. This well-worn practice resulted in stringent Jewish legislation which classified the tax collectors with robbers and bandits. Taxgatherers and sinners were classed together. Luke 5:30.

The unpopularity of publicans in New Testament times is therefore not difficult to understand. They were hated because their methods were necessarily both inquisitorial and arbitrary. (The man who opens your boxes and bundles to appraise the value of what you have, is at best an evil person you tolerate.) The "publican" represented and exercised in immediate contact, at an acute sore spot, the hated power of Rome. The tax itself was looked upon as an inherent religious wrong, as well as civil imposition. Furthermore, the payment of it was considered by many as a sinful act of disloyalty to God.

> The extremists bluntly asserted that any act of submission to Caesar — such as paying a tax — was treason to God. The more responsible leaders did not go so far; yet they looked on the taxes and tolls as tribute exacted by a foreign conqueror, not as a legitimate requirement for the maintenance of social order. Besides, the sums wrung from them were often excessive, to fatten the purses of the Roman officers or swell the profits of the tax farmers.[8]

The taxgatherer, if a Jew, was a renegade in the eyes of his patriotic fellows.

Antipater, or Herod the Idumaean (55-43 BC), played a central role in the Jewish understanding of taxation in Palestine. This Herodian dynasty ruled all or parts of Palestine and neighboring regions from around 55 BC to around AD 70.

> His father, Antipater, had been appointed "governor" . . . of the Jews by the Roman legate in Syria. Antipater's duties had been not much more than the collection of taxes, the religious leadership of the nation remaining in the hands of Hyrcanus as high priest, and the civil administration (courts, police, etc.) probably remaining in the province of the local councils or "elders." A little later, after the victory of Caesar in 47 BC, Antipater was called . . . , and granted Roman citizenship and immunity from taxation. Antipater next appointed his two sons, Phasael and Herod, as military governors . . . the former to control southern Palestine and Jerusalem, the other Galilee. This was Herod's start in life, at the age of 25. Like his father before him, Herod owed his position to his cleverness in playing the game of politics. . . .[9]

Herod the Great (37-4 BC), an able and a constructive ruler, was resented by the Jews for his harsh autocracy. The modest economy of Judea was bent and at last broken under the taxes imposed upon it by a luxurious court and a building program out of proportion to the national wealth. "The burden of such efforts thus fell in two ways upon the peasantry: in taxes, direct and indirect, which made possible the accumulation of funds to finance the building schemes; and in wages low enough to carry them out."[10] Herod was governing a part of the empire for the Romans and he knew it. His duty was to keep the peace and naturalize the Greco-Roman civilization in Palestine. No doubt his crowning achievement was the restoration of the temple in Jerusalem, which must have covered a multitude of his sins in the eyes of his Jewish subjects. Nevertheless, it is no understatement to say that

> All this architectural ambition required money, men, and materials for its realization. Where did Herod get them? The essential question concerns the money. Men and materials were available enough if money was not lacking. There is little doubt that Herod's position . . . enabled him to collect and expend his taxes as he saw fit. In return for exemption from tribute (gifts were not refused), it was incumbent upon Herod to maintain the frontier defenses and internal good government. . . . But that he had every right to collect the taxes, by whatever method and in whatever amount he saw fit, is proved by his voluntary reduction of the taxes by one third in the year 20 BC (the year in which work upon the temple was begun). . . . He expended about what he received; and the largest part of his expenditures was for internal improvements, in Palestine itself.[11]

But the full significance of Herod's building activities was not felt until a decade or more after his death. At the time the religious enthusiasm inspired by the first beginnings of rebuilding the temple served

> to keep the people contented in Herod's days as in the days of Solomon a thousand years before. But the time was to come when the king should die; and then, the secret and growing discontent of those upon whom the burden of taxation fell most heavily becoming longer unbearable, they were sure to rise and voice their wrongs.[12]

The Jews were taxed unbearably to pay for this shrine.

"There were four principal kinds of duties: a land tax payable in kind or in money, a poll tax and a tax on personal property

(Matthew 22:17), export and import customs at seaports and city gates, and in Jerusalem a house tax (Jos. Antiq. 19:6. 3.)."[13] These roused the indignation of all the classes.

Julius Caesar (d. 44 BC) had been lenient toward the Jews but conditions changed under Caesar Augustus (31 BC — AD 14). He sent representatives into all the countries of the subjugated peoples including Palestine to make a list of all persons and their property. It was an enrollment or census for purposes of taxation ordered by the Roman emperor Augustus which brought Joseph and Mary to Bethlehem where Jesus was born. Luke 2:1-7. No discussion of the economic situation of Jesus' day can omit reference to the matter of taxation.

The Palestinian Jew lived under two complete systems of taxation. Each of these systems was designed without regard for the other. In addition to the tribute and taxes due foreign powers, the Jewish people individually were subject to an annual half-shekel payment to the temple. The half-shekel tax (in the New Testament called the *didrachma*) was a symbol of the loyalty of the Jews to the temple during the Hellenistic period. The background of the temple tribute was undoubtedly the half-shekel atonement money required of all males twenty years of age and above. See Exodus 30:11-16. In Nehemiah's time the Jews paid a third of a shekel (Nehemiah 10:32-34) but this was later increased to a half shekel.

The levy was necessary to keep the temple going, for after the fall of Jerusalem in 586 BC, the subsidy from the royal treasury was no longer available. . . . By the time of Christ the tax appears to have been accepted as a matter of course by Jews everywhere. Josephus writes of the collection of this tax by Babylonian Jews and of the precautions they took to get the money safely transported to Jerusalem. The payment of the tax in Palestine itself is reflected in the story about Jesus, who sent Peter to get money from the mouth of a fish (Mt. 17:24-27). Payment had been demanded by officials of the temple who were no doubt sent into Galilee for that purpose. . . . We may assume that such collectors of the temple tax visited every community of Jews throughout the world, beginning in Palestine.[14]

The *stater* coin of Tyre (one *tetradrachm*) was equal to one shekel and paid the temple tax for two persons.

When the temple was destroyed in AD 70, there was no longer a reason for this tax from the Jewish point of view, but Vespasian promptly decreed that Jews should pay two drachmas annually (a shekel was four drachmas) to the temple of Jupiter Capitolinus in Rome. Possibly this was a naive effort of the emperor to develop loyalty to Rome in Jewish hearts, but it produced only bitter resentment.[15]

A coin from the reign of Nerva about AD 97 indicates that the ignominy of devoting the money to support pagan worship had been removed, but that the tax was still being levied during the third century. Eventually it disappeared because inflation made it too expensive to collect.

The native Jewish taxes were for the purpose of religion only, but the oppressive taxes of the ruling power tended to protect and continue foreign domination. But the latter was obnoxious to the Jew and extremely distasteful to the Jewish nationalist. Agitators arose from time to time, like Theudas and Judas of Galilee "in the days of the taxing" (Acts 5:36, 37). "The patriots of Judaism saw but one outlook of promise for the future, national autonomy following liberation from the hated yoke of foreign sovereignty."[16]

The civil taxes imposed by Rome were high and oppressive. According to Josephus, the only thing that the Romans wanted was tribute. ". . . It was partly the method, partly the positive burden, of the taxation which roused the opposition of the people."[17]

For the Jews, the dawn of imperialism, the arrival of the Roman in the Holy Land, was doubly fatal. He brought prosperity, order, peace (in some degree; for Palestine was never wholly pacified); but he also brought a pervasive foreign religion . . . he brought an ever more hated and despised demand for tribute. . . .[18]

"The tribute, first to Herod and his family, then to the Romans, became an unbearable burden, on top of the theocratic tax paid to the Jerusalem hierarchy."[19] According to Frederick C. Grant "the sum total of religious obligations levied upon the people by the various Old Testament codes was nothing short of enormous."[20] In Jerusalem this amounted to a total of "35 percent, not mentioning the 'tithes' to Hyrcanus and his sons!"[21]

> . . . The civil or political taxation was imposed over and above the religious dues demanded of the Jewish nation by the Law. The Law had been established as the theoretical legislation of the priestly theocracy, in which no provision was made for civil or military obligations. *Under the Romans, therefore, there was a twofold taxation of the Jewish people, civil and religious; each of these had been designed without regard to the other, and therefore could not be modified in its favor.*[22]

Grant continues:

> If we may hazard an approximation, where no exact figures are available, *the total taxation of the Jewish people in the time of Jesus, civil and religious combined, must have approached the intolerable proportion of between 30 and 40 percent; it may have been higher still.*[23]

"A twofold taxation, civil and religious, [was] beyond the powers of utmost thrift to sustain."[24] Therefore, no theme was more charged with passion than that of the tribute. When we realize the grinding burden of the Roman taxes and the savagery with which they were collected, the question asked of Jesus ceases to be academic. When we recognize further that the religious taxation

> was designed to be the *sole* tribute of the holy people consecrated to Yahweh; and that the civil taxes, both the Roman and before them the later Maccabaean and Herodian, were *over and above* all these requirements — we can begin to understand how oppressive the whole became. Naturally, the Roman government ignored the priestly taxation, and went ahead just as if the tribute-money were the sole financial obligation of the Jewish nation. Naturally, also, the Jew paid his tithe and his first-fruits and his yearly half-shekel and the other required offerings to the Lord first, before he paid the Roman tax. Hence the imperial tribute was doubly

26

disliked: it was not only tribute exacted by a foreign power, maintaining its authority by brute force — a heathen, "idol-worshipping" empire, whose every existence was a blasphemous denial of the sovereignty of God; but it was tribute levied in addition to the true and rightful obligations of the people, viz., their obligations to their divine King.[25]

Frederick C. Grant rightly observes that the Jew's objection to foreign domination ". . . was not only because of his racial pride or his unconquerable distaste for imperialism" but

> Even more, it was on account of his religion. It was his deepest conviction that Israel could have no king but God — or a ruler directly appointed by Him. If other lords ruled over the people, it was only for a time and as a punishment for their sin.[26]

The Jews of Palestine felt that they were free from obligations to pay the tribute, because the soil of Palestine belonged to God. Rabbinic interpretation never provided for a non-Jewish government within Palestine, nor could it envisage paying tribute to a foreign power. Tribute was seen as a symbol of slavery. In this connection it should be remembered that Rome, too, believed in the inherent right of her own citizens to be free from tribute. For Jewish people, human kingship, especially if it was foreign, implied a denial of the sole rulership of God. Therefore, the payment of tribute was regarded as acknowledgment of Caesar as lord.

> The form of idolatry that was most repugnant to the Jews was emperor worship. Not only was this because the deification of a man, living or dead, was regarded as the height of blasphemy; but, in addition, since the Jews considered Jehovah their king as well as their God, the cult of the emperor-god was also politically objectionable. The inseparability of the political and religious factors is illustrated by Judas, the founder of the Zealots and the leader of a tax revolt in AD 6, who taught that God was the only ruler and lord, and that no threat, not even that of death, should cause the Jews to call any man lord. Accordingly, it need not cause surprise if it is found that the image of the emperor was detested and its introduction into Palestine resisted, even to the point of death.[27]

In his evaluation of the tax revolt by Judas Galilaeus, Ethelbert Stauffer writes: "It is clear that the reason for this refusal to pay the tax was not only an economic protest by a plundered people, not only a political protest by a subjugated nation, but also a theological protest by the people of God against their heathen rulers and their emperor, against 'any confession of Caesar as lord.' "[28] Support for this view is found in Isaiah 45:5, 6, 18b, 22; 46:9.

It is clear that the masses in Palestine lived in considerable poverty and squalor. Taxes were exorbitant and the burden was steadily growing greater in first-century Palestine. The burden continued in an inverse ratio to ability to pay. As a rule the profits of trade went into the hands of a limited number of rich merchants who did not disclose their incomes for tax purposes. Obviously, "the Romans squeezed these profiteers, but they did not put anything substantial back into social services, only into public buildings, and a man like the procurator Ventidius was jibed at even by his Roman contemporaries, who said, 'He entered rich Syria poor, and left poor Syria rich.' . . ."[29] Eventually the crisis reached critical proportions. The grievances resulted in the Jewish war of AD 70.

> The mood of the people, from the time of Pilate (AD 26-36) onwards, was increasingly rebellious. Each succeeding procurator had a harder task on his hands, without being able to cure the root-malady, the economic disease of the time — even supposing him able to discover it. Rebellion came at last. No one in Rome, no one in Palestine had the wisdom to recognize, or could discover the means to solve, the real problem which Palestine faced. The solution adopted was that same blundering, stupid, criminal one which humanity has applied since long before history dawned, namely, Blood and Tears, Murder and Destruction, War.[30]

Taxation Since AD 70

The pattern of taxation continued to be much the same during the history of the early church until the collapse of the Roman Empire. Then, in the agrarian feudal system of the Middle

Ages, taxation underwent considerable change. The assessment of taxes during this period took into consideration both the property owned by each member and his yearly income. Jews were often forced to pay extra taxes. While more onerous, taxes on Jews were, as a rule, not more numerous than those levied on all citizens possessing means. Because land was the primary source of wealth, it became the primary source of taxation during this period. Those who rendered special services to the state were exempt from taxation.

As the constitution of the church more and more assumed the character of a feudal monarchy, ecclesiastical taxation developed in the same direction. Secular rulers paid tribute to the pope in token of feudal allegiance.

During the sixteenth century taxation was used as a method of persecution. For example, special fines were imposed upon the Anabaptists as a milder form of persecution alongside the harsher forms of confiscation of property, exile, imprisonment, and execution. In the seventeenth and eighteenth centuries all Mennonites in the Palatinate were subject to special taxation. Taxes were collected for: (1) attending religious services, (2) being freed from guard duty, (3) as a compensation for exemption from military service, (4) the cost of maintaining the state militia, (5) registration of deaths, births, and marriages, (6) special donations, (7) "protection money," (8) limited toleration, and (9) state church expenses. In various ways, these practices prevailed in many parts of Europe.[31]

Rebellion against arbitrary and oppressive taxation played a major role in modern history. Such milestones in British constitutional history as the Magna Carta (1215) and the Bill of Rights (1689) helped establish the principle of consent and representation in taxation. Much of the desperation that exploded in the French Revolution grew out of one of the most oppressive and inequitable tax systems of all time. In some instances 51 percent of an income was taxed. These exorbitant tax rates were a factor in producing some of the evils associated with the "industrial revolution." Even the postwar taxation of 25 percent of an income in Great Britain during 1926 was considered to be an enormous burden.

During the zenith of European power (1830-70), most nations financed the costs of their wars mainly by taxation. War finance meant in effect retention and increase of the income tax. Some experts maintain that the first income tax appeared in 1799, in England. There the trial period for experimentation with the income tax as a method went beyond its expiration date. It had been introduced to help pay the cost of the Napoleonic Wars. In 1860 it became a permanent part of the British taxing system. Canada imposed a federal income tax for the first time during World War I. All of these seem to indicate that measures instituted by government during war have a way of perpetuating themselves during peacetime.

In the United States, the federal income tax has been the chief source of financial support for the military. This federal income tax became possible in 1913 when the sixteenth amendment to the Constitution was adopted. Prior to that time and as early as 1815, the Supreme Court frequently challenged the constitutionality of revenue acts. However, there have been no serious threats to the income tax as a constitutional tax since the 1913 law. Although much newer than the property tax, it has become the most important federal tax. Authorities believe the Civil War (1861-65) speeded the development of income taxation. The income tax rates are progressive and have been boosted through the years.

The withholding system of taxation was first introduced in the United States during the early forties. At that time the United States government needed additional revenue in order to continue fighting World War II. Some observers call this a restrictive legislation which approaches tyranny in the area of taxation.

Through this indirect method of the withholding tax, which is obviously far more economical than the Roman method, the United States government enforces collection through employers. Money for taxes is taken out of wages. Because the employer has become the unsalaried agent of the Internal Revenue Service, the so-called withholding tax is in reality legal confiscation at the source of the income for every employed citizen (with only a few exceptions). By this clever, indirect way of withholding taxes the government avoids the appearance of tyranny. Although this system has undermined democracy and our sense of responsibility in a subtle way, so far protest to this modern, streamlined form of tyranny has been only minor.

As viewed today, taxes are compulsory contributions levied on private and corporate units to meet the needs of government. They are not a direct charge for special services rendered unless Social Security payments are an exception to this rule since such tax funds are used largely to pay retirement benefits.

In summary, all governments claim a right to the power of taxation. Benjamin Franklin understood this more than 180 years ago when he said: "Nothing is certain but death and taxes." Only recently in human history, however, have governments come to rely on taxes, especially on general taxes levied with the consent of the governed, for the bulk of their revenue. Prior to this it was the duty of unprivileged classes to support the ruling classes. "Taxes as a badge of freedom rather than a mark of bondage are a modern phenomenon."[32]

However, not everyone in our day would agree that taxes are a sign of freedom. Speaking about the questionable national outlook of the United States, Nancy E. Sartin wrote: "In sophistication, we have moved a step beyond Caesar, who conquered to tax. We have learned to tax without conquering, . . ."[33] Basically, war and the fear of war have kept taxes high. Taxes which have been increased to very high levels during a war are seldom if ever reduced to a prewar level. This "perpetual danger" has been observed and reported by C. Northcote Parkinson in his book, *The Law and the Profits:*

> The story of taxation is, broadly speaking, the story of war; and, increasingly, the story of war taxes being retained after the war is over. Of all war taxes, that on income is the most significant. . . .[34]

> In general, as we have seen, the pattern has been for taxation to be imposed in time of war and then retained in time of peace.[35]

An Examination of Biblical Passages Often Used to Justify an Absolute, Unquestioning Obedience to Governmental Demands

There are four New Testament passages which are frequently used in Christian writings to justify an absolute, unquestioning obedience to governmental demands. They are: Matthew 17:24-27; Mark 12:13-17 (with parallel passages in Matthew 22:15-22 and Luke 20:20-26); Romans 13, especially verses 6 and 7; and 1 Peter 2:13-17. While there are, of course, other passages in the Bible which deal with the Christian's relation to the "authorities" (such as Acts 5:29; 1 Timothy 2:1 f.; 1 Corinthians 6:1 f.), those above are referred to in such a fundamental way by many that frequently one receives the impression that these in and of themselves provide us with the definitive Christian point of view. Therefore, with the assistance of numerous biblical interpreters, we will proceed to examine the evidence in each passage in turn.

Matthew 17:24-27

"The half-shekel tax" represented the Temple Tax. Reference has already been made to the historical background of this tax. It dates back to the time of the Exodus at which time it was collected annually by weight from every Jew over twenty years of age. This money was spent for the service of the sanctuary until the first temple was built. In the Diaspora the half-shekel tax became a symbol and an expression of national as well as religious unity.

The conversation between Peter and Jesus probably stems from an occasion when Jesus was asked whether or not He paid the Temple Tax. Jesus answered the taxgatherer's question indirectly by giving an analogy from secular life. It was public knowledge that the Roman government exacted tax and toll from foreigners, but Roman citizens were exempt. Similarly the house of Israel was God's chosen people, His adopted children. Jesus felt that this personal relationship necessitated an inward attitude of the spirit which was incompatible with the compulsory legal payment of a tax for worship. Hugh Montefiore observed that

> Jesus sided with neither Pharisees nor Sadducees. . . . He denied the Pharisees' demand that all were legally obliged to pay the half-shekel. He denied the Sadducees' assumption that free-will offerings were the prerogative of the rich (Mark 12:44). He opposed a tax which did not discriminate between rich and poor, . . . He demanded free-will offerings from all. . . . the main temple sacrifices were paid not by voluntary offerings, but by an imposed tax. It was to this that Jesus was opposed.
>
> And yet He ordered the tax to be paid. . . . To refuse payment would seem to deny the whole Jewish system of worship. This Jesus never did. He pointed to its inadequacies: He insisted on the priority of inward worship over outward observance. He stood here within the prophetic tradition; but, like the ancient prophets, He never directly attacked the cultus as such, only its abuses. To refuse the Temple Tax would be a cause of offence, for it would give the impression that Jesus disapproved of all temple worship. What the Pharisees demanded as a legal due, Jesus gave as a free-will offering of the heart.[36]

J. Duncan M. Derrett takes a different view; he believes Jesus was obliged to pay the tax because He was obliged to save the collectors from the sin of compelling Him to supply the half-shekel. Considering the nature of Jesus' ministry, this is significant and should not be ignored. Moreover, it should be remembered too that in the course of its transmission this story was adapted to the needs of the Christian community at different stages of its history.

For example, after the destruction of the temple in AD 70, the Romans diverted the half-shekel to the uses of Jupiter Capitolinus, a pagan temple in Rome. This proved to be a great problem to both Jews and Christians.

Considering the contrasting situations, J. Duncan M. Derrett declares: "Our pericope proves that Jesus only paid the tax with the *ad hoc* motive of saving the Jewish collectors from sin, whereas this motive could not possibly apply to a collection by Roman collectors for the benefit of Jupiter Capitolinus.[37] Montefiore is in essential agreement when he writes: "The difference between Jesus' voluntary payment of the upkeep of the Jewish temple and the Christian's payment under duress for the upkeep of a pagan shrine is very great indeed. It is almost impossible to see how a story about the former could have been constructed in order to give a precedent about the latter.[38]

If this saying in Matthew 17 was current in the early church in the period before the Temple Tax had been changed into the Roman tax for Jupiter Capitolinus, it must have been understood with reference to the payment of the Jewish Temple Tax by Jewish Christians. Gentile Christians would not have been expected to pay, but presumably Jewish Christians were expected to pay the tax. The story would have been remembered because it gave sanction to the payment of the Temple Tax, not as a requirement, but to avoid offense. This would reflect the period before Christianity had cut its links with Judaism. In the New Testament period it seems that Christians still participated in temple worship (Acts 3:1), and so the tax may well have been paid.

A pressing problem confronted Christians when the Temple Tax became a Roman tax.

> The pericope about the tribute money did not afford sufficient guidance for them, for the tribute money was a secular, not a religious obligation; and it was binding upon all non-Romans without exception. Presumably the pericope about the Temple Tax was included in Matthew's Gospel because it seemed to set a precedent and provide an answer to this perplexing question. If Jesus had paid the Temple Tax not as of duty but to avoid scandal, then Christians, in their situation, must follow His example. They must pay the fiscus Judaicus

to the Roman authorities not because they were legally bound to pay but to avoid the scandal which might be caused by refusal.[39]

Undoubtedly the saying fulfilled a real need in various situations. At the same time we must conclude that its genesis differed radically from its final application.

Mark 12:13-17

The question concerning the payment of tribute to Caesar has parallel accounts in Matthew 22:15-22 and Luke 20:20-26. "Render to Caesar the things that are Caesar's, and to God the things that are God's." Down through the centuries all Christians have found in this verse sanction for a myriad of wrongs.

First, the context of this particular passage is of crucial importance in the understanding of its significance. This incident took place during the ministry of Jesus at a time when there was considerable opposition to Him from the Jews, especially "the Pharisees and some of the Herodians." It should be noted, however, that these two groups held opposite views in regard to the tribute and the Messiah. What strange bedfellows politics makes!

It is clear from the written record that it was their purpose "to entrap him in his talk," thereby driving a wedge between Him and His followers or of getting the Roman government to take action against Jesus as a subversive agitator. Since we know something about the nature of Roman rule and the Jewish antipathy to the payment of foreign taxes, we can well imagine that the tax question directed to Jesus was a highly controversial issue. It was the most dangerous question possible. In a sense, the people were handing Him a live bomb. It appears that Jesus was exceedingly clever in His ability to answer their question honestly while at the same time not arousing governmental action against Himself. Is this why "they were amazed at him" (v. 17)?

After praising Jesus for His impartiality and truthfulness, the Pharisees and the Herodians, who were chafing under the curtailment of Herodian power by Rome, confronted Jesus with their loaded question: "Is it lawful to pay taxes to Caesar, or not? Should we pay them, or should we not" (v. 14 f.)? It was a dangerous question, a cunning and formidable trap. A simple "yes" or "no" answer would have landed Jesus in serious trouble, either with the Jewish people or with the Roman government. Those who were seeking to exterminate Jesus figured that this maliciously framed question could not fail to trap Him. A "no" answer would leave Him at the mercy of the scribes and Pharisees who were wishing to frame Him, while a "yes" answer would leave Him at the mercy of the angry, ultranationalistic Zealots.

Aware of their intention, He said: "Why [do you] put me to the test" (v. 15b)? By asking them to show Him a coin (a Roman *denarius*), Jesus called attention to the fact that the coin bore an image of Caesar — a fact long repugnant to the rabbis who considered such image idolatry, hence a transgression of the second commandment. Apparently Jesus Himself did not possess or use this medium of exchange. At the same time Jesus may have implied that certain Jews were using the services of the government and therefore had obligated themselves. Arthur Harvey takes the position that

> . . . Jesus was giving two answers simultaneously. For those whose loyalty was already given to Caesar as shown by their possession of Caesar's coin involving Caesar's claim to be God — well, of course they had an obligation to pay the tax. For those whose lives were oriented to God, they would not owe Caesar anything. . . .[40]

According to this view:

> The possession of Roman money was not just something forced onto people by circumstances, it was an act which partly defined a person's attitude about God and his ultimate loyalty. Jesus was saying each person would have to decide for himself whether he was a man of Caesar or of God, and make his tribute according to whichever source he valued the most as shown by his style of life.[41]

Or perhaps to indicate that the issue had not been fully or satisfactorily resolved, "Jesus said to them, 'Render to Caesar the things that are Caesar's, and to God the things that are God's'" (v. 17). Not wanting to be cross-examined, Jesus gave a complex and ambiguous answer.

In any case, this was a masterful reply to a tricky question. The professional hairsplitters "marveled greatly at Him." But His answer was far more than the clever footwork of a man in a corner. Not only did Jesus frame the answer in such a way as to avoid having anyone take drastic action against Him (at least temporarily), He also succeeded in putting the issue in right perspective. His reply was more than a clever evasion.

Frederick C. Grant suggests that

> A popular leader and teacher like Jesus would be expected to hold pronounced views on the subject of the payment of this tribute, and His enemies hoped to entrap Him, whatever His views were: if He disapproved, they could denounce Him to Pilate as a revolutionist (cf. Luke 23:2); if He approved, they trusted that this would mark the end of His influence with the people.[42]

"It was clear that Jesus had not fallen into the well-laid trap," comments Ernest R. Bromley, "However, so long as He had not given a 'yes' answer to the question 'Should we pay it,' there was room for the original suspicion; and there was ground for contending that He was in effect forbidding payment of the tax. . . ."[43]

Oscar Cullmann observes that

> As in so many of Jesus' sayings, there is irony in this expression also. . . . The mammon belongs to Caesar: he has had his likeness impressed upon it. So let him have it! But return to God that which is *His* property, what He has given to us. That means: everything, body and soul. Here there can be no talk at all of equality between Caesar and God. The state is nothing final. But it may levy taxes. People should pay these even if it is to the heathen Roman state which has no proper right to the possession of Palestine. Again, in Matthew 17:25 Jesus says that the kings of the earth exact custom and tribute from *aliens*. His disciples should not, therefore, waste their time and energy in resisting the payment of taxes — that is, against the existence of the Roman occupation forces — so long as it is merely a question of taxpaying, of money which indeed belongs to Caesar. But Mark 12:13 has implicit in it this further purport: do not give Caesar *more* than his due! Give him nothing that belongs to God![44]

If ever the State demands what belongs to God, if ever it hinders you in the proclamation of the kingdom of God, then resist it. The whole *Leitmotiv* of the complex New Testament attitude toward the state Jesus formulates here, in this saying.[45]

Jesus' "answers to crucial questions like the one about tribute money to Caesar were not those of a Judas Maccabaeus."[46] At the same time it must be said that

> The answer of Jesus reflects the Maccabean spirit as seen in the canonical Daniel, which finds the unique duty to earthly kings to be resistance to their blasphemous pretensions. In His distinctions between the things that are Caesar's and the things that are God's, Jesus showed that "for Him the foreign emperor was the antithesis of God."[47]

J. Spencer Kennard, Jr., points out that among the Jews the theory of divided loyalty to God and Caesar dates only from early in the third century. Therefore, it would appear that Jesus' attitude and response toward the Zealots is crucial to a proper understanding of the saying about taxpaying in Mark 12:13 ff. We may infer that Jesus was traduced before the Romans as a Zealot, otherwise they would not have crucified Him; but equally we may assume that He was not a Zealot, for otherwise His countrymen would not have preferred Barabbas. On the one hand, Jesus certainly did not regard the state as in any sense a final, divine institution; on the other hand, He accepted the state and radically renounced every attempt to overthrow it. Oscar Cullmann holds that "this double attitude is characteristic of the entire New Testament."[48]

According to Frederick C. Grant, Jesus

> was a revolutionist only in the sense that the ethical principles He advanced were revolutionary in their ultimate effects upon society. For the immediate political future, or, indeed, for the present, He had little concern. The twofold taxation, civil and religious, roused in Him no furious patriotic resentment. "Render to Caesar whatever is his; to God what belongs to Him." The real revolution belongs to God.[49]

In Grant's understanding,

> The innuendo — "to God the things that are God's" — leads our thought off to the far greater reality and overwhelming requirements of the divine sovereignty. In the light of that demand, the lawfulness of earthly tribute becomes a petty question of politics, best settled by acquiescence, since that frees the minds and energies of men for their true task as sons of God and members of His kingdom. If Christ had been a social revolutionary He could not possibly have answered in these words or with the emphasis that they convey.[50]

For Grant, Jesus' answer suggests that "there is no use in trying to avoid payment, as there is in truth no need; it is not a contradiction in terms to pay tribute to both!"[51] But the question remains, Can the issue be resolved so easily? Kennard poses a strong objection to Grant's interpretation.

> Perceiving that Jesus could hardly have felt it a moral duty to support the enslavers of His people, several modern writers have held that He regarded tribute to Caesar as of minor importance compared to service to God. The reasoning they attribute to Jesus is, "Let Caesar have his coins, marked with his own name and picture; God demands quite a different service — chiefly worship and charity. . . . The first is trivial in comparison with the second."[52]

L. H. Brockington too sees this interpretation as erroneous because it leaves "to the reader the burden of discovering which things are Caesar's and which are God's."[53] Kennard is convinced that both parts of Jesus' answer have to do with the question concerning the tribute. The issue of tribute involved the rival lordship of God and Caesar. This was the central problem. To say that only the phrase "Render to Caesar" deals with taxes is to miss the point. "Failure to understand that Jesus could not have excluded the taxes from what belonged to God is a tragic commentary on Christendom's abandonment of Jewish ethical standards."[54]

According to J. Klausner, Jesus "too, felt that the individual was accountable for any gold and silver that he handed over to Caesar. It was the duty of everyone to use money to restrain injustice and to advance righteousness."[55] ". . . He agreed with those who regarded payment of tribute to Caesar as disloyalty to God."[56] Because the true ruler of Palestine is God, His sons are under no obligation to pay tribute to Caesar.

Tribute concerned legitimacy of rule. If God had appointed the Roman emperor to be sovereign over His chosen people, then they were bound to support him with taxes. But if the office Caesar had usurped belonged to God's Anointed, those who supported Caesar were misappropriating the funds that belonged to God.[57]

Kennard observes that as Messiah Jesus could hardly have endorsed the support of a rival king.

Messiahship and refusal of taxes to Caesar were so intimately related that Pilate did not have to concern himself with the second charge, of "forbidding [us] to give tribute to Caesar." It was sufficient for him to extract an admission of the third and inclusive accusation, that Jesus aspired to the throne.

If Jesus had endorsed the tribute, the *titulus* on the cross that set forth the charge might have been "Jesus the Nazarean Prophet"; it could not then have been "King of the Jews."[58]

Therefore, Kennard concludes his book, *Render to God*, with the observation that "In spite of the threefold declaration of Jesus' innocence that Luke puts into the mouth of Pilate, we have every reason for believing that Jesus had encouraged nonpayment of the tribute."[59] This point of view is also reflected by Ernest Bromley:

As long as there was some hesitancy in Jesus' mind over paying the relatively innocuous tax to support the Hebrew temple, it seems as if there would naturally have been a greater hesitancy in His mind over the matter of paying the more weighty taxes due directly to Rome. And the record certainly seems to bear this out. What would Jesus have done after AD 70 when, with the temple in ruins, the temple tax was applied to the support of the temple of Jupiter Capitolanus in Rome? His whole life says that He could not have paid this tax but that had He lived, He would have done as His followers who knew Him best did — refuse to pay it. . . . [60]

Obviously, not all scholars oppose the traditional view that Jesus endorsed the tribute. Nevertheless, those who recognize man's all-encompassing obligation to God would admit the weight of such an interpretation. Jesus' view of life implies a reservation in regard to the state but none in regard to God. For Him there was never any doubt that God was supreme even in the realm which Caesar claimed for himself.

Henry Fast, Jean Lasserre, G. H. C. Macgregor, Ethelbert Stauffer, and Culbert G. Rutenber all provide more extensive helpful treatments of this passage in their respective writings. At this point we will cite only the perceptive insight of Culbert G. Rutenber:

> Jesus is answering a question designed to trip Him up, either with the foreign-hating people or with the Roman authorities themselves. He is confronted with a dilemma which makes it appear that whatever He says He will be wrong. But He refuses to rise to the bait, merely mentioning that both Caesar and God should have what is coming to them. But note what He does not say. He does not say — what Caesar's "due" is — that He leaves an open question. He does not say — how can He? — that Caesar and God are equals, with equal rights to the loyalties of a Christian within their respective areas. He does not even remotely imply that Caesar has any rights that are independent of God and His will. There is only one God and He owns everything. The earth is the Lord's and the fullness thereof; the world and they that dwell therein — including Caesar. Caesar has only such rights as God gives him — and they are forfeit if they violate the rights and purposes of God. [61]

After an examination of the text and its context, it hardly seems fair to say or to imply, as some do, that Jesus' statement in verse 17 supports unqualified obedience to whatever a government requires. To be sure the implication of Jesus' final reply seems to be that men have responsibilities both to persons in government and to God. Jesus did not engage in civil disobedience without good cause.

On the other hand, the total context of Mark 12:17 gives reason to believe that Jesus was making a statement in which the second clause had considerable priority over the first. For Jesus the overarching loyalty was loyalty to God, and it was this loyalty which determined the character of His loyalty to Caesar. When the whole manner of His life is judged it is difficult to escape the conclusion that His supreme loyalty and allegiance were to God. Any conflicting situations He resolved by this primary relationship. As Jean Lasserre sees it,

> Jesus had no intention of putting the emperor's rights and God's on the same level. The emperor's rights flow from the order of this world, and Jesus makes no judgment on them. He seems to be saying: give the same thing to God as to the emperor. But what He means in reality is: above all give God what is His, perhaps in conflict with everything else.[62]

Finally, it is instructive to note that nowhere in the New Testament is the tribute passage cited to defend the duty of paying taxes. The church fathers who quoted it were concerned with the expediency of the payment rather than with moral duty.

Romans 13:1-7

This section of Scripture is undoubtedly most often referred to in connection with any biblical discussion concerning the Christian's relationship to or obligation for government. Apparently this frequent use is caused by either the clarity or obscurity of the passage on the subject. Although the first seven verses deal with the problem of civil authorities, these verses are frequently misunderstood because they are wrenched out of their context, either out of the book of Romans or out of the whole Bible itself. It is not likely that we can understand Romans 13:1-7 properly unless we take into consideration what precedes as well as what follows this passage. Is it not significant that the Apostle Paul prefaces his discussion of "authorities" with a long discussion on the practical implications of Christian love? In fact, he continues on the theme of love to the neighbor again immediately after verse 7. Perhaps if more attention were given to the immediate context, commentators would not find themselves contradicting so many other parts of the Bible.

It is interesting to note that O. Michel believes that there is a lack of connection between Romans 13:1-7 and its immediate context. As a matter of fact he sees the interruption of continuity so serious that he "regards it as certain that 12:21 has its proper sequel in 13:8." One of the four arguments which Michel sets forth for his position is "that the idea of the state with its use of force is far removed from that of love which is the theme of 12:9-21 and 13:8-10."[63] Irrespective of whether or not this section constitutes "an independent excursus," it is instructive to consider why this material might have been placed in such a context. Presumably an author would do this if he thought there was danger that his comments on a difficult issue might be misunderstood. If this was his intention it seems ironic that this is exactly what has happened through the centuries despite the precautionary step.

Many writers of commentaries regard Romans 12:1 through 15:13 as the "practical part" of the book. Even if one should choose to further subdivide this section consisting of four chapters, C. E. B. Cranfield holds that chapters 12 and 13 are intimately related to each other and definitely belong together. He sees no adequate reason for regarding Romans 13:1-7 as in any way an erratic boulder in its context and in one of his books entitled, *A Commentary on Romans 12-13* treated them together. In his preface he declares:

> I decided to stop at the end of chapter 13, because 14:1 — 15:13, while part, of course, of the same main division of the epistle, is of a somewhat different character from chapters 12 and 13. I have naturally been conscious all the time of the fact that no part of Romans can be properly understood except in relation to all the rest of it.[64]

On this matter Jacob J. Enz declares: "No passage in the Scriptures is fully understood apart from the total context of the Bible." Cranfield himself recognizes that Romans 12 — 13 is crucial for Christian ethics:

At a time of widespread uncertainty and confusion with regard to ethical questions, and when the church, at any rate in Britain, seems often only to reflect the uncertainty and confusion of the world, instead of being able to speak a clear guiding word, the choice of these particular chapters for such fuller treatment seemed specially appropriate. Of this at least I am quite certain, that there are few things which could make a more valuable contribution toward the clarification of Christian thinking in the sphere of ethics than would a really serious and patient study of these two chapters of Paul.[65]

Peter Meinhold, who offers a reexamination of the traditional Lutheran position, writes:

It is strange to see how little has been said about the total context in which Romans 13 appears, how little people have taken into consideration the text which immediately precedes and that which immediately follows the words quoted in Romans 13. First of all, it must be stated that the declaration by the Apostle Paul is part of a larger section. It is part of his exposition on the Christian command to love one another. Therefore, Romans 12:21 and Romans 13:8 must be included in the discussion of our passage, for these two verses say that a Christian must "overcome evil with good" and must "owe no one anything, except to love."[66]

In the estimation of Clinton D. Morrison "The whole context of the passage is practical and there appears to be no serious difficulty in stating that Romans 13:1-7 is part of the extended exhortation which began chapter 12: 'Bless those who persecute you. . . . If possible, so far as it depends upon you, live peaceably with all. . . . Let every person be subject to the governing authorities.' "[67] Beginning with Romans 12:14 the attention is shifting from the insiders to the outsiders, to the persecutors, and to the attitude toward the world at large. Then in chapter 13:1-7 we are told about the role of the authorities in the world. Finally, admonitions are given for the community under persecution. The development would hardly suggest that Romans 13:1-7 is an interpolation.

Why is it that in the usual interpretation of Romans 13 a

discrepancy exists between this passage and everything that we know of Paul's attitude? Oscar Cullmann believes that things have come to such a place that men are willing to classify Paul as an almost servile, uncritical servant of any state, as if he would say yea and Amen to every claim of the state, be it ever so totalitarian.

> They base their case on the single Pauline statement in the Epistle to the Romans 13:1: "Let every man be subject to the powers prevailing over us." Few sayings in the New Testament have suffered as much misuse as this one. As soon as Christians, out of loyalty to the gospel of Jesus, offer resistance to a state's totalitarian claim, the representatives of state, or their collaborationist theological advisers, are accustomed to appeal to this saying of Paul, as if Christians are here commanded to endorse and thus to abet all the crimes of a totalitarian state. . . . The fountainhead of all false biblical interpretation and of all heresy is invariably the isolation and the absolutizing of one single passage. This applies most especially to the interpretation of Romans 13:1 ff.[68]

Therefore, Cullmann insists that this passage must be considered together with the other Pauline passages which contain, directly or indirectly, Paul's opinion of the state, such as 1 Corinthians 2:8.

> It is also necessary above all to consider the context of the passage at hand. Even this connection is all too often disregarded. But this context teaches us two things: First, the matter under discussion at this point is the Christian commandment of love — evil is not to be rewarded with evil, rather one is to do good to his enemy. This stands in Romans 12 immediately before the section about the state in Romans 13:1 ff.; and directly afterwards, in verse 8, the same theme is resumed. Second, the expectation of the End is also under discussion: the night is far spent, the day draws near. Rom. 13:11 ff.

> This background to the section is important, and shows in itself that there can be no question here of an unconditional and uncritical subjection to any and every demand of the state.[69]

o   o   o

Hence it is true for Paul also: the Christian is commanded on the basis of the gospel to maintain a critical attitude toward the state; but he has to give the state all that is necessary to its existence. He has to affirm the state as an institution. Of the totalitarian claim of the state which demands for itself what is God's Paul does not speak directly. But there can be no doubt that he too would not have allowed the Christians to obey the state just at the point where it demands what is God's. What we know about his *life,* proves this. He would not have permitted them to say "Caesar is Lord" and "anathema Jesus" (let Jesus be accursed), as this was demanded by the same Roman state to which the Christian is to pay taxes and whose institution he is to acknowledge as willed by God.[70]

Oscar Cullmann recognizes that

> As soon as the state demands more than is necessary to its existence, as soon as it demands what is God's — thus transgressing its limits — the disciple of Jesus is relieved of all obligation to this requirement of a totalitarian state. According to Jesus' command, he is not allowed to give to a state what is God's. But he will not deny even to a totalitarian state those things, like taxes, which are necessary to the existence of any state. We shall see that there was indeed one point at which the Roman state was totalitarian: namely, emperor worship. At this point the disciple of Jesus has to proclaim that the state has transgressed its limits and has demanded what belongs to God; and he himself will not give to the state this which is unjustly required of him. But he will nevertheless pay taxes to it; and he will not take it upon himself in the name of the gospel to proceed against the state by force of arms.[71]

Cullmann's conclusions as given above are acceptable when seen as a whole. Nevertheless, it seems that there are times when even the payment of taxes could be seen as constituting a totalitarian or idolatrous demand of the state. Cullmann does not seem to allow for this possibility. He readily admits that the state should never be "accepted uncritically in all that it does, as if there were no problem at all."[72] He says "that we must remain critical toward every state; that we must nonetheless obey every state as far as it remains within its bounds."[73] Perhaps that is the question! At what point does the state become satanic or demonic in that it is demanding what is God's?

The following quotation from Cullmann shows where he draws the line. For the early Christians, he writes,

> . . . The refusal to offer sacrifice to the image of Caesar and to utter the Kyrios Kaisar had made condemnation to death the compulsory consequence. And every true Christian had to refuse this demand, even if, in accordance with the instructions of Jesus and Paul, he was ever so loyal. They would have acted against the teaching of Jesus and of Paul if they had submitted at this point. If the Roman state had had a loyalty test in any other form than that of emperor worship which was blasphemous for the Christians, the Christians would have been able to meet it in good conscience, and much bloodshed would have been avoided. So long as the state demanded a loyalty test in the form of submission to emperor worship, there could be no peace between Christianity and the state, . . . At this point the Roman state remained continuously, up to the time of Constantine, a satanic power.[74]

This statement from Cullmann makes it abundantly clear that for him an idolatrous confession in words is basically the only thing that matters, not ethics. In other words, it does not really matter what the nature or consequences of the Christian's obedience to the state are as long as he is not asked to say those terrible words which would indicate that a Christian has given up on his loyalty to Jesus as Lord. But for a Christian who takes the ethical dimension of the gospel seriously this difference is of crucial importance. Unless one is alert to the ethical implications of one's acts in relation to the state, a person will repeatedly be guilty of idolatrous devotion to it. Cullmann is aware of the danger but apparently he sees the danger only or mainly on the verbal level. He declares:

> We must resist the totalitarian demand of this state, and indeed at any cost; but only within the compass of this demand. This means: positively, perseverance in our Christian preach-

ing; negatively, perseverance in our refusal of the idolatry demanded by the state. The totalitarian demand we have to resist even to blood; but it is not our business to take the sword, to wage war as the fellowship of Christians against this state in order to destroy its existence.

Cullmann's stance of nonviolent resistance seems commendable, but his lack of moral discernment as to what constitutes idolatrous loyalty to the state is questionable. Although states frequently do require verbal loyalty oaths of a totalitarian type, most states are willing to forego that formality if they have the assurance that the money and the lives of their respective citizens are subject to their undisputed direction and control. But this "hidden" type of idolatry is precisely where the greatest danger lies. Caesar is not God. Caesar (the state) is a human being, and yet he wants to be worshiped as God in the confession and obedience he demands of his subjects. In terms of Old Testament thought, human kingship usurps the place which belongs only to God.

Herbert M. Gale offers an intriguing solution to the problem in Romans 13:1-7. He found striking similarities between some biblical passages dealing with government and its functions and other passages concerned with the Law. Because these similarities indicate a kind of parallel thought, Gale contended that Paul's thinking concerning the Law provides the clue for a clarification of his thinking concerning the state. Both: (1) are divinely instituted, (2) serve the primary function of restraining wrongdoing, and (3) are transcended or superseded by the way of love.

It is hardly accidental that immediately after Romans 13:1-7 there follows exactly the same kind of thought and language which, in Galatians 5, follows Paul's arguments regarding freedom from the Law. "Owe no one anything, except to love one another; for he who loves his neighbor has fulfilled the law" (Rom. 13:8). The commandments, he writes again, "are summed up in this sentence, 'You shall love your neighbor as yourself.' Love does no wrong to a neighbor; therefore love is the fulfilling of the law" (Rom. 13:9 f.). . . . Paul . . . is saying that just as love transcends or supersedes the Law, so it transcends or supersedes the function of the state in the matter of wrongdoing.

o o o

The most important fact which needs to be noted is that when Paul writes of that which has been divinely instituted, he does *not* mean that such a so-called divine institution should be understood in any *absolute* sense. The Law was for him, as previously indicated, such a divine institution. This does not mean, however, that the Law is given the "last word." . . . Yet this Law, now negated, *was divinely instituted*. In other words, for Paul, "divinely instituted" simply does not mean "possessing final and absolute authority."

When Romans 13:1-7 is read in the light of this clearly evident distinction, the major difficulty in the passage vanishes. Since "divinely instituted" in the case of the Law does not mean "possessing final and absolute authority," it is absurd to insist that it *does* mean this in the case of the state.

      o   o   o

Altogether, in view of the way in which Paul thought in regard to the Law, it must be concluded that when he writes that the state is divinely instituted he does not mean that it possesses final or absolute authority, or that the Christian owes it an unqualified loyalty and obedience.[76]

At this juncture it should be pointed out that there were already in the Old Testament clear examples of institutions regarded as divine and yet not having final or absolute authority. The monarchy, for example, was viewed as "a divine gift" but it was also regarded as the source of much evil and distress. Furthermore, kings, like Saul who was represented as "Jehovah's anointed" and Nebuchadnezzar who was spoken of as "my [God's] servant," (Jer. 43:10a), were also portrayed as having sinned in more ways than one.

Therefore, Paul was not deviating from Old Testament precedent when he thought of an institution which, although established by God, did not possess complete authority. For Paul, as for the prophets, kings and nations serve God because He is the Creator and Ruler of history. God appoints and uses rulers for His own purposes irrespective of whether they are good and ideal or not. Paul was not affirming any specific divine action in favor of Rome. Rather he was suggesting that whatever agency is ruling, it is within the divine ordering. It is being used as God's instrument for the maintenance of order in society. John Howard Yoder penetrates to the core issue when he says:

49

Paul was simply arguing that the Christians in Rome should not rebel even against a government which threatened to mistreat them. They could be confident that God was using the powers in and behind the state within His providential purpose. The state is not instituted, i.e., established, but rather accepted in its empirical reality, as something that God can overrule toward His ends. Paul therefore does *not* mean that in the divine acceptance of the state there is implied any ratification of its moral standards or political purposes, or any theory of the proper state. The Christian is called not to *obey* the state, which would imply actually receiving from the state his moral guidance, but to *be subject*, which means simply that he shall not rebel or seek to act as if the state were not there. Whether he obeys the state or finds that his submission must be in the form of disobedience and accepting punishment for it, will depend on what the state asks of him.[77]

But in no situation should a person be required to disobey conscience in submitting to government. Without being or becoming a violent rebel the Christian can refuse to do what he regards as wrong, but he must patiently endure the consequences. To resist with respect is to render a service to the state by reminding it of its true function.

Peter Meinhold too declares that Romans 13:1 ff. "is not a passage in which every governmental action is given *carte blanche* or in which every possible claim of a state is unconditionally recognized. We misunderstand the meaning of these words if we interpret them in this way."[78] At another place Meinhold writes:

Nevertheless, the Christian must recognize the state as long as it functions properly. That does not mean that a Christian must always be obedient to the state. It is by no means self-evident that a Christian recognizes the state a priori. If the Apostle Paul asks Christians to recognize the state, he is merely thinking of the conditions in the Roman congregation of his time. . . .[79]

Clinton D. Morrison provides further clarification regarding this relationship in his book, *The Powers That Be*:

As it is for conscience' sake that the Christian is subject to the *exousiai,* so it is for conscience' sake when he asserts his freedom from them. . . . his conscience alone would determine his subjection to the state or his noncompliance with its demands.

Exception to the Christian's responsibility to be subject to the *exousiai* is only a question of noncompliance for conscience' sake. . . . Paul leaves no doubt whatever that the primary thing is the fulfillment of the Christian's calling, obedient service to Christ. This may be expected to lead to suffering, at times for civil disobedience. But nowhere does noncompliance or even suffering for that matter, possess any merit of its own. While the church had no reason to live in fear of civil officials, it was greatly to the advantage of the Christian mission not to provoke the state needlessly. . . .[80]

Cranfield believes that the Christians of Rome did pay taxes, and the real ground of their doing so is their knowledge of the place of civil authority in the divine purpose. Therefore, Paul appeals to their actual practice, reminding them of its true significance. In all this it is apparent that the early church had an amazing ability to fuse ethics and eschatology, in a way which seems inexplicable to modern men characterized by greater logic but less lively faith. Notice the movement of thought in Romans 13 from respect for government to love of neighbor and then to watchfulness because the Last Day is at hand.

Yoder and Cranfield suggest that in Romans 13:7 we have depicted the kind of attitude which Christians are to manifest in their relations to various types of people. This means discrimination: giving to each his due but not giving everything to government as is often assumed. If "taxes," "revenue," "respect," and "honor" do not all refer to government, then Yoder feels that Christians have grounds for exercising discrimination. In his estimation, reverence and fear certainly are not due to government. Accordingly, it can be said that Romans 13 provides textual grounds for questioning any government on the propriety of the requirements it makes of its citizens. Verse seven sums up the section and says specifically, not that we are to render to government what it asks for, but that we are to give to each what is due. It seems extremely likely that Paul intended this to be a commentary upon the "render to Caesar" passage in the gospels, indicating precisely that not everything belongs to Caesar. What then is Caesar's due? Lasserre contends:

> That there is no question of loving the state; only the totalitarian state demands a devotion bordering on love. That is the very way in which it is pagan, because it is arrogating rights it does not have, and misunderstanding its true vocation, which is to be the servant of God, and only that. So there is no question of loving the state, nor worshiping the emperor who embodies it, but only of showing it "a simple, responsible and resolute attitude." What we owe it is the tribute, respect, and honor. . . .[81]

John Howard Yoder believes that

> We are not called to submit to every demand of every state. When Paul instructs the Roman Christians (Rom. 13:7) to give "tax to whom tax is due, toll to whom toll, respect to whom respect, and honor to whom honor," this is the opposite from saying that tax, toll, respect, and honor are due the state. He is saying, as the similarities to Mt. 22:21 and 1 Pet. 2:17 confirm, that we are to discriminate and give to each only his due, refusing to give to Caesar what belongs to God.[82]

Lasserre, like F. J. Leenhardt, is convinced that it is in the essence of a state to be totalitarian and demonic. Moreover, the texts in Romans 13 and Revelation 13

> referring to these heavenly powers which rule the authorities present them precisely as hostile to Christ; this is a fact, I think, which has not been enough stressed. So if these texts do concern the state, it must be admitted that most of them show it to us in a pessimistic and pejorative light, in an atmosphere far removed from the serene collaboration between church and state which is too often, and wrongly, seen in Romans 13. For "let every soul be subject to the higher powers . . . which come from God" must surely be interpreted in the light of all these texts which talk of the political demonic powers; and this will modify its meaning.[83]

52

The fact is that since Constantine Christians have tended to think if a state no longer persecutes the church, that is a sure sign of its being a just state. Contrary to the testimony of the New Testament, they have a prejudice in favor of the state, which goes to the point of passive and unconditional obedience to it. But because the state does not persecute the church, can one really conclude that the state is faithful and has not been "demonized"? Is it not equally possible that the state is well and truly demonized, but does not persecute the church which grants it all it wants, and is in haste to satisfy all its whims, like a mistress afraid to lose the favors of her rich, protective lover? The fact that a state does or does not persecute the church could never be a sufficient criterion in itself for judging whether that state is "just" before God. There is no more a "just state" than there is a "just war"; all that scholasticism is irreconcilable with the Bible's message.

"We wrestle . . . against principalities, against powers, against the rulers of the darkness of this world, against spiritual wickedness in high places," wrote Paul (Eph. 6:12); and we know now that these authorities he speaks of are the political authorities. The first Christians actually lived within this terrible struggle; almost all the New Testament heroes were imprisoned, tortured, or condemned to death. But have these words still a significance for us today? For centuries we Christians have denied it, turning upside down the gospel message: "We must strictly obey the principalities and powers, and must serve them faithfully. . . ." In Protestant theology Romans 13 has eclipsed Ephesians 6:12: it is surely obvious that our traditional perspective is distorted. What tribute have the churches paid, then, to enjoy such a peace? Might it by any chance be in their submission to military service?[84]

Or to make the question relevant to our particular study, might it be in their submission to paying taxes for war? In conclusion we can consider Cullmann's striking statement found in *Christ and Time*:

The Christian believer will always place over against the state a final question mark and will remain watchful and critical, because he knows that behind it stand powers which do indeed have their place in the divine order determined by the victory of Christ, but which nevertheless for the time being still have a certain possibility of permitting their demonic strivings for independence to flare up into apparent power. . . . In spite of all the positive statements of Romans 13:1 ff., the state here, as in the entire primitive Christian conception, is not an ultimate but only a penultimate institution, which will vanish when this age does.[85]

1 Peter 2:13-17

This segment concerning civil powers, embedded in a section on duties of Christians in the world (2:11 — 4:11), bears a significant resemblance to Romans 13:1-7. It is possible that both Peter and Paul were drawing from a common source.

Apparently Peter was writing to Christians who were either experiencing or anticipating persecution. In such situations the basic element which is to characterize the Christian's attitude and action is subjection, submission. However, submission as it is used here must not be confused with passive obedience. The purpose of government is (negatively) to suppress evil, and (positively) to encourage good. The supreme example of Jesus is introduced to provide an effective guide for Christians. Suffering is inevitable because the authorities are not naturally just. Nevertheless, Christians must endure these persecutions, not in a spirit of resignation or rebellion, but by devoting themselves to prayer and to witness. They are called to suffer, but not to inflict suffering. The context speaks of nonviolent love to neighbors and enemies. Unconditional love to all men, yes, but not unconditional obedience to any government. The absolute and perfect subjection is to God and this servanthood gives no room for wickedness.

"Honor all men. Love the brotherhood. Fear God. Honor the emperor." This verse (17) provides a striking parallel with Romans 13:7 which also contains four commands. Moreover, it is likely that there is also a connection with the words of the Lord: "Render to Caesar the things that are Caesar's, and to God the things that are God's." Here, as in the saying of Jesus, the debt to God is mentioned distinctly as well as the debt to the emperor. Martin Rist finds that the meaning of the verse in 1 Peter is more explicit than it is in Romans. Peter's doctrine that the emperor is to be honored and obeyed as a representative of God implies that he is not to be regarded or worshiped as a god. "Not only does the author insist that Christians be good citizens in all matters of conduct, but he concludes his exhortation with the specific warning that although they are to fear (i.e., worship) God, they are merely to honor Caesar (1 Peter 2:17)."[86] Worship belongs to God and to Him alone. C. E. B. Cranfield believes that

> It is noteworthy that in 1 Peter 2:17 the wording of Proverbs 24:21 has been significantly altered. In Proverbs we have: "My son, fear thou the LORD and the king"; but in 1 Peter two different verbs have been used, presumably in order to avoid using the same verb to denote what is owed to the emperor and what is owed to God. God is to be feared . . . and the emperor honored.[87]

A survey of usages in the New Testament confirms the suspicion derived from 1 Peter 2:17 that the term "fear" is not characteristically used of what is due to an earthly ruler. It is interesting to note that

> in every instance of a positive command to fear with a personal object expressed, apart from Ephesians 5:33 . . . , God or Christ is the object. . . . In Romans 13:4 "the power" is no doubt the object to be supplied; but in this case we have a command addressed to the wrongdoer, not a general command. Nowhere in the New Testament is there a general exhortation to fear . . . the civil authority.[88]

This has great significance for understanding how the Christian should relate himself to governments. According to Peter's point of view "The Christian's obedience to the state ceases where the disobedience to God begins."[89]

Undoubtedly it is significant that Peter and Paul, who recommended submission to the "authorities," both died as martyrs at the hands of "kings." This fact alone speaks volumes and serves as an eloquent testimony of how the Christians understood their role in relation to the state.

Paul, who for conscience' sake obeyed the authorities as far as he possibly could, was persecuted and executed because, for conscience' sake, he refused them obedience.[90]

Paul was not afraid of reminding Christians why they could not be perfectly conforming subjects of the Roman Empire, obeying any decree of Caesar regardless of what it demanded of them. As a "citizen of heaven," he knew that their first obligation was to conduct their lives in a manner which would match their citizenship. This was their highest loyalty.

An inclination to read the Bible too literally, coupled with a disregard for the historic background of the times, can sometimes prevent us from properly understanding the meaning of some biblical incidents and/or texts. Moreover, to understand the New Testament message properly we need also to consider carefully other passages such as Acts 4 and 5 and Revelation 13 and 19 where the institution of government is viewed more critically. In any case, a healthy balance is needed to protect us from using biblical references to justify an attitude of indifference to the war tax problem.

Argument Against
the Payment
of War Taxes

War taxes are those taxes which a government collects explicitly for the purpose of financing some current military operation or generally those tax funds which are used for the payment of past, present, and future wars. This definition suggests that the taxes can be both direct and indirect in nature. The 10 percent "Defense Tax" of 1941, the 5 percent "Victory Tax" of 1943, the 10 percent Federal Excise Tax on telephone service (reinstated in April of 1966), and the Vietnam surtax of 1968 would serve as examples of the direct tax because they are "more nearly an out-and-out war tax than most taxes."

However, "Income Taxes," collected from citizens individually through the Internal Revenue Service, might also qualify as direct taxes for war because a large percentage of money collected in this manner (approximately 60 to 75 percent in the United States) is devoted to military preparations. The personal income tax is the United States government's largest source of income.

The following comments and quotations will seek to "spell out" a Christian basis for the nonpayment of war taxes. The grounds for such a position can be considered under three major points:

57

The Christian's Obligation to Obey God Rather Than Man

The question of God's sovereignty in the affairs of men is the crucial point of departure. From the Christian point of view, God's place in the lives of men must always take priority over any human obligation. He is the supreme ruler of history and deserves our unqualified obedience. Whenever there is a conflict of interest between God's purpose and man's this ought to be resolved in the reality of His lordship over our lives. Jesus Himself made this clear by placing the obligation to the state always in the context of our obligation to God.

According to the Bible, God always expects men to give Him priority in every decision. If there is a conflict between what men expect of us and what God expects of us there should be no question about our ultimate and primary commitment to God. This despite the contention of governments that the claims of religious freedom or conscience are not feasible. He deserves first place in our life. Such a commitment implies the willingness to disobey existing laws within the society. This was clearly the decision of the early church as it is recorded for us in Acts (5:29). "But Peter and the apostles answered, 'We must obey God rather than men.' " The original Greek implies an either/or, not a both/and condition. The nation-state, no less than the individual, is ultimately subject to the sovereignty of God. No government has the authority to abrogate the right of individual conscience. When the claims of government violate the claims of God, then the claims of government must yield. A totalitarian demand for that absolute allegiance which is due to God alone is the kind of obedience which the Christian cannot and should not give. To comply would constitute "an act of idolatrous worship." As someone once said: "I refuse to accept what is unacceptable to the Creator of this universe."

The Christian's obligation to obey God rather than man is intimately related to his exercise of religious freedom. Since there are persons who object on religious grounds to supporting or financing military operations in any form, it is believed that such persons are denied the free exercise of religion (guaranteed by the First Amendment to the Constitution) when forced to pay income taxes used for military purposes.[91] Just as there are provisions for conscientious objection to military service, so there should also be provisions for conscientious objection to making atomic bombs and missiles or paying for the making of them. Internal Revenue law, in effect, prevents the free exercise of the religion of most pacifists. This is true for the simple reason that it requisitions over half of the tax dollars for military purposes.

Christians, moreover, are not obligated to participate in acts which violate their consciences under God. Norman M. Thomas is one person who understood this truth very well. With the title of his early book he posed the rhetorical question, *Is Conscience a Crime?*

> This assertion of the right of the individual to refuse obedience to the state even in the emergency of war or to lay down limits to which his obedience must be confined is the essence of conscientious objection. . . . Its significance does not depend primarily on the reasoning power of the objectors or their personal ability or their character — important as these matters are — but in its existence as a practical affirmation that under certain circumstances civil disobedience may become a duty for which men will dare to suffer.[92]

When men have faith in a "higher law than man's" they not only have the right, but the duty, to disobey existing laws which contradict the will of God. Presumably Alfred Hassler is correct in stating that "a government that actually believes in freedom of conscience should not put men in prison for practicing it."[93] In his book, *The Challenge of Asia*, Ralph Borsodi affirmed that ". . . it is usurpation, not legitimate government, for any government to use its coercive powers to compel individuals to pay for, and to acquiesce in, measures for their alleged welfare in which they may not individually believe.[94]

Apparently Governor Osborne of Kansas understood this matter in a similar manner. In his message to the legislature on January 15, 1874, he proposed an amendment to the existing law which required a special tax for the nonperformance of military duty (the tax referred to was the thirty-dollar fine payable each May for the privilege of exemption from military service). Speaking of the desirability of securing Mennonite immigrants for Kansas the governor said:

It is hoped that large accessions may be made of these worthy settlers, and it may properly be considered whether any class of people who are conscientiously opposed to bearing arms should be compelled to pay an onerous tax to be relieved therefrom. It strikes me as incongruous that such religious convictions should be made taxable by our laws.[95]

In response to the governor's recommendation, the legislature repealed the "onerous tax" on March 9, 1874.

A Christian is by his acceptance of God's sovereignty required to resist every human authority except those that seem to be the proper instruments of God's will for him. Christians cannot equate obedience to the state with obedience to God. As an Anglican archbishop in South Africa once declared: "It has been the traditional teaching of the Christian church that there is no obligation on a man as a Christian to obey unjust laws."[96] On the basis of the total biblical message it would appear that civil disobedience is a valid expression of Christian love and concern. Dwight Y. King, for example, illustrates the necessity for disobeying government when he reflects on the problem of a religious selective service objector whose conviction is not recognized by the government.

> In this situation, can I a conscientious objector counsel my friend and neighbor to violate his conscience and enter the military service? It seems to me not. Yet in this act of encouraging my friend to resist the draft (even though doing so legally in the courts), I have violated the present law by counseling my neighbor to obey God rather than men.[97]

Except in a few instances, persons are born and automatically become citizens of certain countries in the world. But everyone in a sense has the opportunity of deliberately choosing to become a "citizen of the world." This should commend itself to Christians who seek to worship and serve the God whose children we all are.

The Christian's Commitment to Love Rather than Hate

Here we are concerned with the question of man's ethical responsibility to others. By what right should any government expect a Christian to contribute to a cause which contradicts so flagrantly what he believes most firmly, namely, that his life is to be used to help other people but never to destroy them? It has been suggested that the most complete violation of Christian love is the waging of warfare, a highly organized effort to destroy the property and take the lives of the so-called "enemy" nation. The application of this to the war tax problem suggests that where persons love their fellowmen and are neighbors to all, this basic orientation to life rules out the possibility of doing injury to others or of destroying the lives of others. Christians must choose "Life which is life indeed" or they shall be guilty of choosing death, not only for others, but also for themselves.

War inevitably inflicts death upon others. Then if the life of Jesus provides moral guidance for this world, Christians are obligated to endure suffering rather than to inflict it upon others, just as Jesus did up to His death on the cross. From this perspective it could be concluded that Christians cannot pay war taxes. To do so would seriously compromise their commitment to God as revealed in Jesus. As citizens of God's kingdom of love there is no other choice.

> Since God wants His stewards to help Him in the development of His world, and in advancing His creation, man cannot help in needless destruction of property and lives. He can have no part in devastating wars that ruin cities, destroy industries, and snuff out the lives of millions of innocent people, to say nothing of the aftermath of moral and spiritual degeneration that follows war.
>
> In the summer of 1948, with a group of college students, I was looking over the hundreds of acres of twisted steel, crumbled concrete, and pulverized bricks of what was once the beautiful city of Hamburg, Germany. Now for miles not a building was standing and we were told that under the rubble were buried 55,000 bodies. Turning to the boys I remarked, "We certainly did a good job of it." One of the boys countered, "I claim no part in it. I thank God I was a conscientious objector."[98]

It would appear that such a declaration of noninvolvement has integrity only if Christians refuse to pay the war taxes which most governments require of them. Christians can hardly claim to be innocent of the devastating consequences which war brings upon people if they readily cooperate with governmental demands for war tax payment. Such involvement betrays the claim to right action and implicates Christians in the horrors of modern warfare. These acts are *our* acts unless we take a stand against them. In other words, we are not true conscientious objectors to war until we disassociate ourselves from the payment of war taxes. To take this course of action will not necessarily prevent the government from collecting the money, but at least a Christian witness will have been made. As Milton Mayer once said, with the Aesculapian oath in mind: "We hope to do good, under no circumstances do we intend to inflict injury or do harm."[99] The present situation offers a startling contrast, however.

> The amount Christians pay for things they know are absolutely evil is frightening. In 1957 *The Christian Evangel* estimated (conservatively so) that the 8,800 Amish Mennonites of Elkhart County (Indiana) were annually paying *three million dollars* toward future wars just by paying taxes![100]

In 1959 it was estimated that "the average American family pays $850 per year for military defense through taxes."[101] The staggering size of current appropriations for defense is clearly an index of national reliance on military might. Isaiah's woe (31:1 f.) directed against those who "trust in chariots" is not without relevance in our own day. This prompts one to ask in what way payment of war taxes constitutes cooperation with an evil system. In complying with the taxing powers of the war-making state, are we not helping the whole military establishment to run smoothly,

> helping thus, to force it on millions of youth and, thus, in turn, promoting war — taxes being an integral part to any war.[?] Does not our acquiescence . . . help to create the impression at least of outward unanimity, the impression that there is no real opposition? It has become obvious that the absence of active dissent is an objective the Johnson administration had tried assiduously to achieve. In this state of affairs, civil disobedience may be the best way to practice reconciliation. Insofar as we help to smooth the way for American militarism and the regimentation which accompanies it, we are

certainly not practicing reconciliation towards the millions of people in the poor and nonwhite countries against whom American war preparations, . . . are directed.[102]

Does nonresistance to evil mean that we should cooperate with it?

> The government of a nation may be said to declare war and to wage war, but in fact every gun "it" shoots, every bomb "it" drops, every ship "it" sinks, every battle "it" wages, is shot, is dropped, is sunk, is fought by individual human beings.[103]

James Russell Lowell (1819-91) possessed keen insight on the subject of war:

> "Ez fer war, I call it murder, —
> There you hev it plain an' flat";[104]

The personal character of all war, even in an impersonal age of technology, is further substantiated by John E. Steen's observations on the subject of "Death and Taxes":

> If you were handed a gun, right now, and told to shoot a man — or to drop napalm on a village — you couldn't do it. Not without being stripped of your normal feelings and trained to kill.
> But the same good people, you and I — who would vomit at the sight of burning flesh and blood on our hands — have no qualms paying taxes for somebody else to kill and burn. . . .
> . . . We see glimpses of the horror our tax money buys. But it all seems so far away. Not quite real compared to what we know of life here. If we are forced to face the issues — we make excuses. . . .
> The managers of the Empire will let us speak — as long as we hand over the young men and the cash. And we are afraid to refuse. . . .
> . . . And now we too are slaves of the Almighty State. . . .
> The government could never get away with murder — in Vietnam or anyplace — without our help. The War Machine must be fed warm bodies and cold cash by the millions. . . .[105]

Therefore if personal responsibility has any real significance the

Christian can see no alternative but to refuse to cooperate with the tax collecting system under present circumstances. Unless followers of Jesus dissent from paying war taxes, how are government leaders to know that Christians are opposed to making war on other peoples whom God has created? Confrontations at the Pentagon would be another way, but perhaps nothing makes the point as clearly as does tax refusal.

Hans A. De Boer is one of those who has discovered the significance of the smallest act.

> During the four years of my travels round the world, in every single place where I went, the fearful word "war" was hanging over men's heads like the sword of Damocles, ready to drop at any moment, killing and destroying. No power on earth would be sufficient to portray all the misery and distress, the hunger and death which men have brought upon their brothers. I should have despaired if I had not ever and again come upon men who had placed all their strength in the service of reconciliation. It is not always those important people who guide the nations, whose names shine like jewels out of the wilderness of human unreason and wickedness — it is often unknown persons, those who have taken seriously the commandment of God, who have become witnesses in a world which is lost, and who alone have the power to change that world.

> If there is one thing I learnt on my travels it is this: the humblest sacrifice, the smallest act often bears more weight than those decisions of which the whole world speaks. The latter may control the destiny of nations, uproot millions and conquer great countries, but the former conquer the hearts of men. . . .

> I had left on a mission for my firm, but I returned in the service of a higher Power, which stands above all force. . . . I am thankful for all my experience, and I see in it a commission to pass on to others the message of the obligation of love.[106]

The Christian's Duty to Give Rather Than to Take

The question of man's stewardship is not incidental to the war tax problem. Rather it suggests what the basic issue really is.

Paying war taxes simply does not add up to responsible Christian stewardship. Let us explore the reason for this.

If a person is morally responsible for the expenditure of *all* the money that he earns or receives, does it not get in the way of complete and total stewardship to say that there is a certain percentage of his income (determined by the government) for which he is not responsible? Is the Christian simply to hand over to the government whatever amount of money it asks for, irrespective of what it is used for? Can the Christian wash his hands of the matter and say that the government alone (even in a democracy) is entirely responsible for how the money is spent?

First of all, let us consider the second half of Jesus' answer in Mark 12:17 which made tribute an issue of stewardship. According to Kennard,

> When the purpose for which taxes were used was righteous, payment was service to God Himself. But Jesus insisted that those who paid the tax be responsible for what was done with the money. It was God's, not theirs to employ as they saw fit.[107]

> Judaism taught that "taxes payable by Jews in the Holy Land were God's property." To take what belonged to Him and give it to Caesar was dishonest.

> God's claim to the taxes rested upon His title to all material possessions. . . . The principle of God's ownership is asserted often in the Old Testament. . . .[108]

This is evident in Exodus 9:29; 19:5; Psalms 24:1; 89:11; 104:24; 1 Chronicles 29:11-16; and Haggai 2:8 where it is suggested that the whole earth belongs to God and all the things which are in it. Everything belongs to God.

> All of Israel's financial activities were based on the concept that God is the owner. Josephus observes, "Now there is no public money among us except that which is God's." . . .
> This sense of stewardship of God's possessions is a distinctive mark of Judaism. . . . Because the handling of wealth was not subject to fickle personal choice, misuse of it invoked severe censure by the community. . . .

The pious Jew was obligated not only to handle God's property with discretion, but also to safeguard it from seizure by God's enemies. Scripture left no room for a competing claimant. Heathen kings like Ben-hadad, who dared to say to Israel's ruler "Thy silver and thy gold is mine" (1 Kings 20:3), incurred divine chastisement. . . . . To obstruct payment of tribute to Caesar was to obstruct brigandage.[109]

Lester E. Janzen once wrote: "Your money is you because it represents what you are and have done. Something of you goes where your money goes."[110] Your money is part of your life. It represents your energy, your purpose, your life.

If the Christian is a steward of all of God's gifts to him, how is it possible for him to relinquish responsibility for the use of taxes collected by the Internal Revenue Service when he knows full well that most of that money is going for past, present, and future wars? Does the state have a right to determine how the Christian's financial resources are used, especially when they flatly contradict all the purposes to which he has dedicated his life?

In our day the execution of war depends not so much on the conscription of men as on the conscription of money. Money, not manpower, is "the central vital nerve of the military Leviathan." It takes vast sums of money, secured through the Internal Revenue Service, to purchase and maintain the enormously expensive push-button weapons. Preparation for full-scale war in our day calls for drafted dollars rather than drafted men. The Federal income tax is the chief link connecting each individual's daily labor with the tremendous buildup for war. Therefore, paying taxes is a little like making a purchase. The only difference is that in this case the purchase is war preparations.

During the days of World War I, Pastor John Franz and members of the Bethlehem congregation near Bloomfield, Montana, were severely criticized for their refusal to take part in the war. Specifically, they were asked why they refused to buy war bonds. In responding to this challenge Pastor Franz tried to explain that

. . . Christians really own nothing. We are here to take care of all God's things. Since our money is God's money, we can

66

use it only for things that please Him. We cannot buy war bonds, because that makes war possible. Using our money to make it possible for others to be killed would be just as wrong as going into the army and killing a man ourselves.[111]

In light of the above, how can a Christian voluntarily or willingly give money to a tax organization when he knows that this means that almost as much will in effect be taken from the suffering peoples of the world? Not only would such cooperation reduce the help available to those who need it but it would substantially increase the suffering for many. It is said that 10 percent of our gross national product is spent on war every year while hunger, poverty, and overpopulation abound both at home and abroad. In addition there will be the risk of contributing to a thermo-nuclear world disaster. Those who think that "concern for the eventual use of this money finds no support in Jesus' teaching"[112] should consider Kennard's argument based on the biblical materials given above. In a similar vein James C. Juhnke writes:

> Let's not kid ourselves that we are not responsible for our tax money. No miracle happens as my money travels from my home to Washington, D.C., to transfer responsibility for what I did from myself to the government. I know that 75 percent of what I sent in will be used for military purposes. And I know that it would not have been used in this way if I wouldn't have sent it.[113]

Speaking about the murder resulting from government-financed wars, James Russell Lowell did not hesitate to identify the party ultimately responsible:

> Guv'ment aint to answer for it,
> God'll send the bill to you.[114]

Consider the terrible discrepancies between what the Christian in America hands over to pay for wars and what he gives to heal the wounds of the world. This is enough to shake a man's conscience if he has a sense of responsibility for the way he spends his money as well as the way he uses his life. In 1968, Daniel Zehr declared:

Canadian and U.S. Mennonites are paying an estimated $417 million in individual income tax a year. Of this amount, approximately $227 million is used for defense expenditures.

º   º   º

The annual U.S. and Canadian expenditures of $97.2 billion on defense dwarf the gross budget of the United Nations. Secretary General U Thant has proposed a budget of only $141 million for 1968. It is instructive to note that the figure needed by the United Nations is less than the amount paid for military purposes by the Canadian and U.S. Mennonite tax payers. *Thus the Mennonites alone contribute more to the cause of violence and destruction than is used by the largest organization in the world devoted to peace.*[115]

This kind of a contrast prompted Roy Pearson to confess that stewardship "is a fearfully neglected aspect of the Christian gospel in our time." Listen to his reflections:

One day I read that the national budget proposed for 1958 called for expenditures of $71.8 billion and that "items related to present and past defense" composed 80 percent of it, "leaving about $14 billion for all other federal activities from combating floods and narcotic smugglers to minting pennies and keeping up the price of peanuts." I thought of a man I know who has an income of $10,000 a year, who pays an income tax of $2000, and who gives $300 to the church and various charities. Eighty percent of his income tax presumably is spent for national defense. That means that $1,600 of his money goes for bombs and bayonets and $300 for preaching and teaching; $1,600 for poison gas and hand grenades and $300 for cancer clinics and mental hospitals; $1,600 for submarines and aircraft carriers and $300 for social workers in the slums and chaplains in the prisons. And then I asked myself, is this simply "too bad"? Is this just "a necessary evil"? Is this nothing more than another burden which we have to carry because of Russia's threat to our security: Or could it be that this is sin against the God who put within the reach of man the iron and the steel which, shaped now into swords and spears, was meant instead for pruning hooks and plowshares?[116]

President Eisenhower aptly summarized the human problem implicit in the huge United States military budget. On April 19, 1953, he said:

Every gun that is made, every warship launched, every rocket fired signifies, in the final sense, a theft from those who hunger and are not fed, those who are cold and not clothed. We pay for a single fighter plane with a half-million bushels of wheat. We pay for a single destroyer with new homes that could have housed more than 8,000 people.[117]

War taxes are a waste. The vast sums of money which the United States government spends yearly for defense purposes is frankly astounding. It seems incredible that a "civilized" government like the United States can be persuaded so easily to take on the burden of additional taxes in order to pay for the ghastly business of slaughtering more and more people in Vietnam. Those who try to live their lives in obedience to the ethical mandates of the Christian faith are agonized by the disastrous consequences of this "budget of death." The money and energy which is put into this "budget" is even more impressive when one considers how little real security this gigantic expenditure provides. The fact that the United States economy of abundance is built largely on a "military-industrial complex" threatens the welfare and security of individuals, not only in the United States, but of people around the world. The military system is economically and inherently wasteful. What responsible purpose can such colossal waste possibly serve, especially when money for education, housing, medicine, and general economic development is needed so desperately in many areas of the world?

Why should any government inflict so much suffering upon countless innocent people not to mention the tremendous waste of tax funds? Charles A. Wells, noted journalist and editor of *Between the Lines*, pointed out the extent of military waste already evident in the forties and fifties:

> The cost to the American tax payer . . . has been beyond calculation. Billions of dollars' worth of planes, tanks, and ships have been rushed to completion under the drive of a propaganda-inspired hysteria that Russia was about to attack — equipment that became obsolete soon after it was commissioned for service. Thousands of planes produced that have never flown, tanks that proved fit only for training purposes, ships that had to be "modernized" at a cost of additional

millions soon after launching. These expenditures covered far more than the defenses needed to protect our own shores and to strengthen our friends.

Proof of this profligacy is found in the Hoover Commission estimate, of 1948, that over 11 percent of our military spending is wasted in inadequate planning, duplication of management, and the general profligacy of military institutions. An additional 10 percent wastage from losses in obsolescence, due to the rapid advance of military technology, would be a most conservative estimate. The military have not permitted estimates of these losses to be published, but it is known for instance that $2.5 billions were spent on the controversial B-36 bombers which were so speedily replaced by the B-47s and the B-52s. Because of inadequate planning, whole jet squadrons were junked before being commissioned. No tour of United States air bases, tank and artillery centers, or Navy shipyards can leave doubt of this enormous waste.[118]

According to C. Northcote Parkinson, "Waste, like taxation itself, has its origin in war."[119] Surely this is a burden which no one should be asked to support, especially not those who are conscientiously opposed to it. According to a Christian understanding of God's purpose in this world, it would appear to be an unjust tax law which compels men to contribute money to a government which is currently spending most of its resources to destroy the lives and property of others.

Historical Survey of Nonpayment Positions and Practices

Even though the current concern about war taxes and the protest movement against payment of the same is only about twenty years old, this is not the first such movement in history. In fact, nonpayment has a long and even honorable history. Christians since the time of the early church have been troubled in conscience over the demands which governments have made upon their possessions for questionable ethical purposes. Jean Lasserre admits that the Christians of Rome to whom Paul directed a letter

> were probably tempted, like anarchists of all ages, and as the context clearly indicates (verses 6 and 8), either to commit ordinary offenses against the law, such as slanders, perjuries, violations of local laws, refusals to pay tribute, insubordination by slaves, etc., or else to be disrespectful to the Roman political authority, discreetly to make light of the laws and have a generally scurrilous attitude. But Paul can scarcely have thought they would go so far as to . . . take part in "plots against the security of the state."[120]

But early Christians definitely refused to pay taxes to Caesar's pagan temple in Rome. For them it was clearly a question of idolatry. Only God could be worshiped.

Historically, Anabaptists and Mennonites have taken their tax paying obligations to governments rather seriously. In Switzerland it was said of them that "they owed no allegiance except to pay their taxes."[121] Undoubtedly this attitude was due largely to a rather literal reading of the Bible. However, the Hutterites of the 16th century held a strong position for peace which included the nonpayment of war taxes. For them this was a pressing issue. Franklin Hamlin Littell records that

> The Hutterites criticized their Anabaptist confreres, the Swiss Brethren, because they mixed with the world and made no Christian distinctions regarding war taxes . . . and "close practice" in commerce. . . .[122]

"The Swiss Brethren refused to bear arms but paid war taxes, for which the Hutterites criticized them."[123]

The Anabaptist community in Moravia was experiencing considerable pressure from King Ferdinand "for financial and direct military support against the Turks."[124]

> Since the Anabaptists were committed against warfare or furnishing funds for it, they faced the dilemma either of sacrificing their principles of faith or of refusing obedience to the government at a time when the cry arose, "The Turk is marching upon Vienna!" In addition, the Moravian diet had pronounced all those as dishonorable who managed to be released from these taxes.[125]

The differing convictions among the Anabaptists regarding the payment of special war taxes led to the Nikolsburg disputation of May 1527. This major event in the history of Anabaptism in Moravia occurred simultaneously with the arrival of Hans Hut who found that "there were already in the neighborhood some who were trying to practice community of goods, who rejected the magistracy and refused to pay taxes for war, in spite of the nearby threat from the Turks."[126] "The propriety of paying taxes for military purposes in defense of Christendom"[127] was one major area of disagreement between Balthasar Hubmaier and Hans Hut. Hut, in contrast to Hubmaier, was not willing to support political rulers, especially when they asked for money to outfit their armies against the Turks.

In Nikolsburg Hubmaier led a group ("Schwertler," *q.v.*) who paid the tax and approved the use of the sword in self-defense against the Turks, while the opposing group ("Stäbler," *q.v.*) were negative on both points. In 1511 the "Pikard" in Austerlitz declared they could not pay the war taxes, which were against their conscience. The agreement of Nov. 26, 1556, between the Palatine and Hutterite Anabaptists in the region of Kreuznach stipulated the following regarding the payment of war taxes: "But what is blood money, and serves wars or other unrighteous things or undertakings of the government out of itself and not out of divine orders and thereby attacks the conscience, the God-fearing man is not obliged to pay them, because God demands of him that he love his enemy (Mt. 5; Rom. 12), and the God-fearing man has promised this to God, and he shall not make any weapon that serves only that end (Is. 2; Mic. 4), that the God-fearing man may not be a partaker in their wickedness or blood guilt.

The Hutterites consistently refused to pay war taxes and special levies. Peter Riedemann's *Rechenschaft* of 1545 says on this point: "For war, killing, and bloodshed (where it is demanded especially for that) we give nothing, but not out of wickedness or arbitrariness, but out of the fear of God (1 Tim. 5) that we may not be partakers in strange sins."[128]

Emperor Rudolph II had asked for war contributions but the Brethren very decidedly declined, accepting all the consequences. Many were killed or dragged away into Turkish captivity. The "Stäbler" Anabaptists finally left the area under the control of Lord Liechtenstein and moved to Austerlitz where they were received by the "four brothers of Kaunitz" who willingly agreed to their articles "concerning war and war taxes."[129] It is thought probably that the thoroughgoing and courageous opposition of the Hutterites to war taxes may have influenced the Quakers in this regard.

The Anabaptists and other despised and persecuted Christian sects of humble people originating in central Europe in the second quarter of the sixteenth century, by upholding their rights of religious freedom based on biblical and reformation teachings, were of vital importance in paving the way, through Baptists, Quakers, and others, for our American religious freedom. . . . There were different groups, but they were one in teaching the supremacy of the individual conscience even when it ran counter to the orders of the state. . . .[130]

As long as "Christians may provide money by way of taxation," the pacifistic Polish Brethren of the sixteenth century observed, "there will never be a want of soldiers."[131]

One of the clearest and most appropriate instances of war-tax refusal appears in the stand taken in 1637 by the relatively peaceable Algonquin Indians in the face of taxation for armaments by the Dutch. After having sold arms to the Iroquois Indians, William Kieft tried to pacify the offended Algonquins by improving Fort Amsterdam which he claimed was to provide protection for Algonquins as well as for the Dutch. When he sent his tax collectors to the Indians they were met with a storm of resistance: "Protection indeed! His fort was no protection to them. They had not asked him to build it, and were not going to help maintain it."[132]

The earliest refusal to pay taxes by Friends was probably in 1660-1702 in England when they withheld tithes for the support of the established church. This practice also carried over into America.

The American Quakers made refusal of war taxes an integral part of what was undoubtedly one of the most potent witnesses for peace and against war in any age by any people. As early as 1711 William Penn informed the queen that his conscience would not allow "a tribute to carry on any war, nor ought true Christians to pay it."[133] Then in 1715 an anonymous Quaker writer spoke with even greater certainty in a pamphlet entitled *Tribute to Caesar*.

> To pay ordinary taxes is justifiable, of course, and it is not always necessary to inquire what the government does with them. But when taxes are levied specifically for war purposes, and announced as such, the Christians must refuse to pay them, says the author. Hence the expedient of voting money "for the queen's use" in response to a demand for military aid is a sacrifice of principle.[134]

John Woolman (1720-72) admitted that paying taxes "for carrying on wars" gave him a scruple which he never could get over. He could see no effective difference between actually fighting a war as a soldier and supporting it with taxes. In his *Journal,* he wrote:

> To refuse the active payment of a tax which our Society generally paid was exceeding disagreeable, but to do a thing contrary to my conscience appeared yet more dreadful. . . . Thus, by small degrees, we might approach so near to fighting that the distinction would be little else but the name of a peaceable people. [135]

During the French and Indian War in 1755, Quaker tax refusers, including John Woolman, John Churchman, and other Friends, drew up an "Epistle of tender love and caution to Friends in Pennsylvania," which said in part:

> And being painfully apprehensive, that the large sum by the late act of Assembly for the king's use, is principally intended for purposes inconsistent with our peaceable testimony; we therefore think that as we cannot be concerned in wars and fightings, so neither ought we to contribute thereto, by paying the tax directed by said act, though suffering be the consequence of our refusal. . . . Though some part of the money to be raised by the said act is said to be for such benevolent purposes, as supporting our friendship with our Indian neighbors, and relieving the distresses of our fellow-subjects, . . . we could most cheerfully contribute to those purposes, if they were not so mixed, that we cannot in the manner proposed, show our hearty concurrence therewith, without at the same time assenting to . . . practices, which we apprehend contrary to the testimony which the Lord hath given us to bear. . . .
> Our fidelity to the present government, and our willingly paying taxes for purposes which do not interfere with our consciences justly exempt us from the imputation of disloyalty. [136]

The War of the Revolution brought serious problems, owing to the Society's antiwar convictions. The Friends were sympathetic with the desire of Americans to obtain redress of grievances, but most of them remained neutral so as to avoid all warlike measures. They provided the first considerable group of "conscientious objectors" in our history. As they refused to serve in the army or militia, they were frequently suspected of Tory sympathies, and their property was seized to

pay for substitutes or lost by their refusing to pay war taxes.
. . . Fines against them for various charges involving their
patriotism amounted during the war to about £ 35,000. [137]

Rufus M. Jones estimated the property loss to Quakers at not less
than 50,000 pounds. [138] The high regard in which Quakers were
held by the fathers of the republic, in spite of their failure to
give more active support to the war for independence, is significant.
At the same time, it must be admitted that not all Quakers refused to perform military duties.

> During the early years of the war many were expelled
> from the Monthly Meetings for paying war taxes, or placing
> guns for protection on their vessels; for paying fines in
> lieu of military service or in any way aiding in the war
> on either side. [139]

It was their faithful witness against war taxes, however, which has
helped to keep the issue alive to our day. Anthologies by Staughton Lynd, Peter Mayer, and Arthur and Lila Weinberg all provide significant documentary material for closer examination.

The Mennonites held principles similar to those of the Quakers
regarding war. In fact the majority of them were opposed to the
war taxes as well. Klaas Reimer, a Mennonite minister of Danzig
and later of Molotschna (1805 f.), "was opposed to contributions
made to the Russian government during the Napoleonic War." [140]
For the most part Mennonites during the American Revolution
(1776-83) held firmly to their principle of nonresistance. Nevertheless, public pressure was used to persuade citizens to join the
"Associations," the term used to refer to companies of volunteer
soldiers.

> Special taxes and fines were . . . imposed upon the mem-
> bers of this religious group during the Revolution for their
> pacifist views. Some paid these and rendered noncombatant
> service. Others served prison sentences rather than contribute
> in any way to the cause of war. [141]

In a special petition, the Mennonites and Dunkards assured
the Colonial Assembly of Pennsylvania in 1775:

it being our Principle to feed the Hungry and give the Thirsty Drink; — we have dedicated ourselves to serve all Men in every Thing that can be helpful to the Preservation of Men's lives, but we find no Freedom in giving, or doing, or assisting in any Thing by which Men's Lives are destroyed or hurt. [142]

The war taxes and the fine for not joining the Associations presented a difficult problem to the Mennonites and other nonresistant groups. They had held the principle that they should pay taxes without question, assuming that in so doing the government became responsible for using the money properly. The Quakers generally refused to pay these taxes, although when the government seized their property in payment they offered no resistance. It is not certain how most of the Mennonites met this problem of fines and special war taxes. The records show that some of them paid these levies. In Montgomery County, Pennsylvania, the majority of the ministers opposed the payments. Bishop Christian Funk insisted these taxes should be paid. The resulting controversy led to the formation of a schismatic branch of the church. The Funkites continued as a separate organization until 1850 when they became extinct. [143]

During the Civil War (1861-65), American Mennonites for the first time faced conscription. A variety of responses was made to the draft situation because the regulations were not the same for each state. In some cases an "exemption could be obtained by furnishing an acceptable substitute or by paying $300 for the hiring of one. Naturally conscientious objectors were not satisfied with this law, for it seemed inconsistent to hire a substitute to fight in one's place. [144]

"In October, 1862, the Southern Confederacy passed a law exempting the conscientious objector from the draft provided he furnished a substitute or paid a tax of $500 into the public treasury." [145]

In both the North and the South the Quakers objected to the commutation fee since they considered it a tax to obtain religious liberty which was their inherent right and therefore should not have been offered for a price. The Mennonites did not object to the tax, apparently not opposing conscription as such but only conscription for military service. [146]

History would seem to substantiate the opinion that Christians, not excluding the peace-loving Mennonites, have always been more inclined to hire soldiers to work in their place than to do the actual fighting and warring themselves. Apparently, this alternative does not prick the Christian conscience as much.

In Richard B. Gregg's book, *The Power of Non-Violence*, there is an account of a tax refusal on a mass scale in the old Austro-Hungarian empire during the mid-nineteenth century. The emperor Franz Josef tried to subordinate Hungary to the Austrian power, contrary to the terms of the old treaty agreement between those two countries. Although the Hungarian moderates felt helpless in the face of such a threat, Francis Deak, a Catholic landowner of Hungary, challenged them to protest against the injustice and oppression.

> Deak proceeded to organize a scheme for independent Hungarian education, agriculture, and industry, a refusal to recognize the Austrian government in any way, and a boycott against Austrian goods. He admonished the people not to be betrayed into acts of violence, nor to abandon the ground of legality. "This is the safe ground," he said, "on which, unarmed ourselves, we can hold our own against armed force. If suffering must be necessary, suffer with dignity." This advice was obeyed throughout Hungary.
>
> When the Austrian tax collector came the people did not beat him or even hoot him — they merely declined to pay. The Austrian police then seized their goods, but no Hungarian auctioneer would sell them. When an Austrian auctioneer was brought, he found that he would have to bring bidders from Austria to buy the goods. The government soon discovered that it was costing more to distrain the property than the tax was worth.[147]

Numerous attempts were made by the Austrian government to wear down the tax resistance of the people. As a consequence the jails were filled to overflowing. Other strategies, including conciliation and compulsory military service, were tried. But the Hungarians persisted in their refusal to obey. Finally, on February 18, 1867, the emperor capitulated and gave Hungary her constitution once again.

Henry David Thoreau (1817-62) was the American pioneer

of "civil disobedience." The term was coined by him and dates back to 1849. He was imprisoned for refusing to pay taxes to the United States government which upheld slavery and which was carrying out a war to conquer Mexico. Thoreau published a justification of his position in 1849 entitled *Resistance to Civil Government*. He said: "If a thousand men were not to pay their tax bills this year, that would not be a violent and bloody measure, as it would be to pay them and enable the state to commit violence and shed innocent blood."[148] Thoreau stated a crucial question for his day and for our day, and his answer deserves all the emphasis that can be given it.

> Must the citizen ever for a moment, or in the least degree, resign his conscience to the legislator? Why has every man a conscience then? I think we should be men first and subjects afterward. It is not desirable to cultivate a respect for the law, so much as for the right.[149]

The effectiveness of Thoreau's nonviolent resistance was probably demonstrated most clearly by two men in the twentieth century, namely, Mahatma Gandhi and Martin Luther King, Jr. Thoreau once said: "If in a country the government acts wrongly, then a prison is the only place a self-respecting citizen can live in."[150]

Leo Tolstoy (1828-1910), a master of the religious basis of pacifism, understood that the implications of conscientious objection to war included the problem of war taxes. Here is an illustration of his universality and insight.

> "You may wish to make me a participator in murder; you demand of me money for the preparation of weapons; and want me to take part in the organized assembly of murderers"; says the reasonable man — he who has neither sold nor obscured his conscience. "But I profess that law — the same that is also professed by you — which long ago forbade not murder only, but all hostility also, and therefore I cannot obey you."[151]

Gandhi (1869-1948) was an effective practitioner of civil disobedience in India. According to him noncooperation involves four stages of which only the last one consists in refusal to pay taxes, which is in fact a form of civil disobedience. . . .

He sees two degrees in civil disobedience. The first is "defensive disobedience," which is an involuntary and reluctant disobedience to laws which are intrinsically bad and whose observance would be incompatible with self-respect or human dignity. . . .

The second degree is "aggressive and offensive civil disobedience," symbolical of a revolt against the state. It is disobedience to laws which may be just in themselves. He gives as an example refusal to pay taxes, and adds: "This offensive civil disobedience, either on the part of individuals or the masses, is a very dangerous weapon although it is the most effective of all the peaceful weapons at our disposal."

The integrity of those who use it must be proportionate to this danger. It is scandalous to see it used by hotheads or violent people.

Although consisting in a revolt against laws which may be intrinsically just, disobedience may be morally justifiable, because every other means having been considered, it is the only nonviolent way of combating an unjust government. The morality of such conduct is that of a "just war," with this surprising factor in its favor — that it does not involve violence and its evil consequences, and that it is directed towards peace by peaceful means.[152]

A. J. Muste (1875-1967) was considered to be the outstanding spokesman in the United States for the Christian pacifist position. It was his conviction as early as 1936 that the most effective thing which people in the world could do was "to dissociate themselves completely from war." Muste struggled intensely with the war tax problem, refusing since 1948 to pay Federal income taxes. Moreover for years he articulated the position that there should be alternate provisions "to making H-bombs or paying for the making of them." Consequently he repeatedly challenged the right of the government to tax him for waging war. He said:

The two decisive powers of government with respect to war are the power to conscript and the power to tax. In regard to the second I have come to the conviction that I am at least in conscience bound to challenge the right of the government to tax me for waging war, and in particular for the production of atomic and bacterial weapons.[153]

In the past decade the Church of the Brethren has tried to help its members arrive at a Christian position on war taxes. In 1960 Dale Aukerman and others issued a declaration of income tax refusal which read in part as follows:

We reject, as blasphemy against Christ, the prevailing readiness to exterminate hundreds of millions, or even all mankind, in order to "defend our values, our faith." Since modern technological warfare is much more dependent on huge amounts of money than on manpower, we believe that refusal to turn over our bodies is not enough; we can no longer turn over our dollars for the present rush toward mass annihilation.[154]

Since 1963 or earlier, noted folk singer-pacifist Joan Baez has refused in several ways to pay her income taxes. One year she refused to pay the 60 percent of her income tax which finances war and armaments. The government then confiscated the amount from her bank without her consent. In another year she filed a claim with the IRS for a refund of the 60 percent. She added the following personal remarks:

I am not interested in having the money for myself, and neither do I want it to be spent on destruction, torture, and death in the name of Freedom, Democracy, Christianity, or any other name we may use to justify murder. When the words God and Country are linked together, I feel that they are meant to be in that order. God is not a God of murder, but of love, and so accordingly, and in the name of God, should our nation begin to act as well as preach.[155]

During the past decade or more Mennonites, Brethren, Quakers, and others in North America have become increasingly disturbed over the large percentage of income tax money which is used to finance past, present, and future wars. Because of various levels of understanding and the complexity of this ethical issue, a variety of responses has been made to it. Following is a classification of seven general positions taken: (1) reduce taxable income by increasing benevolent contributions to 30 percent; (2) pay the taxes willingly without questioning the use of the money; (3) pay the taxes voluntarily, but express a protest to the government; (4) reclaim the "war tax" funds from the Internal Revenue Service by completing and filing *Form 843* if caught in the tax withholding system; (5) voluntarily limit your income so you need not pay; earn a nontaxable income; (6) refuse to pay all or part of the taxes as a witness and a protest; (7) refuse to file or pay. Concerned persons who take any of the above positions can and should simultaneously work for an alternative "peace tax." Individuals who refuse to pay taxes (in part or totally) frequently send an equivalent amount to peace and service agencies like Church World Service or UNICEF of the United Nations.

The Peacemaker Movement is clearly the "veteran" in the area of war tax refusal. For twenty years they have been saying "no" to conscription for war and making the alternatives known to others through their publication, *The Peacemaker*. They have also printed a *Handbook on Nonpayment of War Taxes*,[156] an extremely useful source of concrete information about what has happened to other tax refusers in their efforts to witness for peace and against war.

During 1960-61 the Pacific Yearly Meeting of Friends circulated a proposed bill offering an alternative to persons conscientiously opposed to the use of income taxes for military purposes. Such persons would be given the opportunity of designating their tax money to a special "Civilian Income Tax Fund." This fund would go annually to support the United Nations International Children's Emergency Fund (UNICEF). It was suggested that the individuals in question would also pay an additional 5 percent above their normally computed tax as a proof of their sincerity.

The Church of the Brethren has also invested time and effort into a nonmilitary arrangement for paying taxes. It has been suggested that the simplest procedure would be for the IRS to accept checks drawn to specific nonmilitary accounts. Obviously, the only alternative payment which would mean anything at all in the realistic sense would be an alternative payment to some program outside the budget of the government. Otherwise, this would be a bookkeeping transaction only.

Many people who are disturbed about tax refusal have grave reservations about any form of civil disobedience. To such it must be observed that civil disobedience to the demands of government has been a long and honorable tradition among Anabaptists and Mennonites. This was true in relation to both their personal involvement in actual warfare and in the payment of war taxes, but especially in their refusal to take part in military efforts. Dwight Y. King observed:

> In World War I, hundreds of Mennonite young men resisted, violated the law, and accepted the consequences, rather than violate their consciences by accepting the law's required induction into the armed forces. Our opposition was no less great in World War II, but we managed to gain provision, by law, for conscientious objectors. This development brought about a shift in Mennonite behavior from resistance and civil disobedience to cooperation with the government through alternative service programs. [157]

Since we are aware of the great cost in conviction and action which was required of conscientious objectors to war during World War I before draft alternative provisions became a part of law, it is hardly realistic to think that an alternative to military taxes will be achieved more easily. The militarists say: "Yes, you may protest paying for bombs and battleships all you want, just as long as you keep on buying them by paying your taxes to the IRS." It is the experience of men who know political realities that government officials are usually not too much concerned about individuals who are, after all, willing to go along with the system even though that may be under protest. This suggests that an alternative arrangement for a peace tax will have a remote chance of becoming law only if there are a sufficient number of men like A. J. Muste, Ernest Bromley, Maurice McCrackin, and others who see the issues clearly enough, who object strenuously to the present system, and who are willing to take the risks of this position regardless of the consequences.

It is believed that a substantial number of tax objectors of this kind could exercise a significant witness effect because it would challenge certain functions of government as wrong even for legitimate government. According to John Howard Yoder, this strategy would have the further advantage of concentrating first, not on the search for an alternative to war taxes, but of finding an effective way of giving

> a testimony to the inappropriateness of what government does with our money. If we waited for a smooth and legally irreproachable way of making such a statement, before trying to make it with the means now at our disposal, we would in effect be saying that the statement is not very pertinent. This would be similar to the French Mennonites, who say that they will be conscientious objectors as soon as there is a good conscientious objection law, but that meanwhile they do not find it necessary to suffer for their convictions. Should means of alternative payment be proposed by the government as a result of the impact of tax objections by numerous Mennonites, this would in a sense weaken the protest but only by government's admitting something of its moral validity. If on the other hand we ask for the procedures to be smoothed out first we are making no protest at all.[158]

"As a preliminary to the basic issue of tax objection," John Howard Yoder has

> pointed out that there is something very questionable about the willingness with which Mennonite Church agencies by withholding from their employees' income serve as arms of the federal government for tax collection, which thereby relieves the individual of any conscious choice concerning the bulk of his tax money. If we had different convictions concerning the relationship of church and state, or if we had no moral questions about the validity of the nation's expenditures, or if we were not specifically church agencies, the issue would not be as important; the combination of these various factors makes the entire practice really questionable. We would object to the state's collecting taxes to support the church; yet without compunction we let church agencies collect to support the state.[159]

Are Christians aware of the incongruity of this action? To overcome the difficulties of collection, the government has impressed employers into its service as involuntary and unpaid tax collectors. This is a form of conscription. The fact that it is practically impossible to be employed unless one submits to the withholding tax has put such pressures on the vast majority of citizens that objection or refusal to pay tax for the sake of conscience means the loss of a job without much hope of finding employment elsewhere. Therefore, it would seem that the use of the employer in the collection of taxes is immoral because it puts the taxpayer in jeopardy if he uses his citizen's right to object. Moreover, the government's use of the church as a tax-collecting agency is an encroachment upon religious liberty. Should not this loss of human freedom be rectified?

Conclusion

Caesar has often been an enemy of the church. He may in our day become a more dangerous enemy than he has ever been before. Nevertheless we have it on the highest authority that we are to love our enemy.[160]

That, I believe, is both an astute observation and a tremendous challenge. It recognizes the tension and conflict which often exist between the church and Caesar and the fact that the Christian struggle with Caesar is to be carried out on the level of self-giving love and redemptive suffering.

Is it possible that our reluctance or failure to see the ethical discrepancy in war tax payments means that we are motivated primarily by the fear of men? Are social displeasure, inconvenience, financial loss, and the possibility of legal punishment more influential in determining our course of action than loyalty to the kingdom of God? Could it be that many of us Americans find it difficult to make a genuine Christian commitment because we enjoy too much the fruits of the system of which we are a part? Have we been "accomplices to crime because we whispered when we should have shouted"?[161]

Neither industry nor the Pentagon is primarily responsible for creating a monster military machine out of a peaceful American democracy. The United States spends seventy or eighty billion dollars a year on the means to make war, because its citizens want it that way, or at least care too little to protest.

The chief purchase of our incredible wealth has been arms. If, as we believe, we are not an aggressive people, our epitaph may be that this nation built the greatest military machine in history out of public apathy and political inertia.[162]

Almost every citizen, or at least every family, once a year makes a personal contribution to the moral and financial support of the military monster — one of the idols of our time. This gesture of support for war is carried out every time a person forwards a share of his earnings to the government. But why should any person, on receipt of the government's demand for money to kill the innocent, hurry as fast as he can to comply? Must Christians pay to have innocent persons killed? Instead, why should they not indicate their unwillingness to pay for war? Would Jesus expect them to do less? True, the government might still succeed in getting their money by attaching checking accounts or by confiscating personal property, but at least they would have made their witness against a powerful and dreadful evil. Ted Webster warns us: "There is a world of difference between handing war tax money to IRS without question and making them come seize it."[163]

A statement on nuclear power prepared and adopted by the General Conference Mennonite Church meeting in Bluffton, Ohio, during August, 1959, indicates a clear awareness of our involvement. It declares:

We are too much involved in these pagan practices. Our silence in the face of these and other social evils condemns us. Our taxes support gigantic armaments programs. Our economic prosperity rests too much on these cold-war tensions. We are so entangled in all these sub-Christian trends that we cry out for light and for the leading of the Lord. Our devotion to God's great purpose in Christ Jesus is often feeble. We find it so hard to put our faith into action.[164]

Perhaps the reason Mennonites were so shocked by the "fantastic military installations in the very heart of the nation" was due to the fact that it helped them to understand clearly what became of their tax money. "Sin is sin," we say. "It will destroy a people which condones it. We oppose the use of any of God's natural resources for the purpose of warfare with our fellow men."[165] But having made our pious declaration we go right on paying the war taxes which make the sin we detest possible. What will it take to convince us of the fact that this is idolatry in the sight of God? When will we decide not to give to Caesar the things which belong to God?

Perhaps the answer is to be found in a joint historic peace church pronouncement of 1954 which begins with the words: "No man can serve two masters. . . ." and then concludes with the appeal: ". . . Let us be done with these fearful weapons, regardless of what others do. . . ."[166] Is not this the solution if our responsibility belongs first to God and our fellowmen and not to any state? Certainly the Christian cannot agree to offer to God merely those services and funds "which remain after the state has made its claims and demands on the individual."[167]

But one question at least persists in the minds of the people: Is not the refusal to pay war taxes too negative an act? Why should Christians create "trouble" in their community in this way? Let it be said that the Christian's objective in refusing to pay taxes is not to bring about an unnecessary disturbance, but to make a necessary witness to others by being faithful and obedient to God's purpose for men in this world. As Christians we are called to testify that "Jesus Christ is Lord" in every area of life. If our primary task is "to be living evidence that God is intervening among men to change the structures of human relationships," both personal and social, then it would appear that it matters greatly whether we are obedient in doing what we know to be right, irrespective of whether or not tax refusal sounds like a negative act. Daniel Slaubaugh expressed it very well when he said: "I am not so important. But everything which I do is *very* important."[168] It has been pointed out that in his own day the prophet Jeremiah appeared to be very negative in his criticism of Judah. And yet who is to suggest that Jeremiah's perception of the total situation was incorrect? He saw the evils for what they were and had the courage to say so. But despite his negativism, Jeremiah was positive. When the city of Jerusalem fell in 587 BC and the situation was most hopeless, Jeremiah had the courage to go out and buy a piece of land. What a positive witness that was! Dwight Y. King asks:

> Is it not conceivable that there may be times when the refusal to compromise, the refusal to be satisfied with any of the apparently available alternatives is the most true and faithful and ultimately effective thing a Christian can do? Will sane and committed men at times feel constrained to disobey the law out of a sense of obedience to a higher allegiance? At least to hundreds of history's most revered heroes, not to serve the state has appeared the best way to love one's neighbor.
>
> The Christian's living testimony will sometimes be that of signs. What matters about such a deed is not whether it is effective, not the changes it immediately brings about in the social order, but what it signifies. Since we are not the lord of history, might not there be times when the only thing to say is a word to which no one seems ready to listen; yet it needs to be said nonetheless, in the confidence that it is our Lord and not we (and our eloquence, effectiveness, etc.) who will make of our sign a message? Perhaps this is what D. Bonhoeffer had in mind when he wrote:

> One asks: What is to come?
> The other asks: What is right?
> And that is the difference
> Between the slave and the free man.[169]

Dwight Macdonald's argument on the responsibility of individuals versus the responsibility of peoples is persuasive. Using the atomic bomb to illustrate his discussion he wrote:

> Insofar as any moral responsibility is assignable for The Bomb, it rests with those scientists who developed it and those political and military leaders who employed it. Since the rest of us Americans did not even know what was being done in our name — let alone have the slightest possibility of stopping it — The Bomb becomes the most dramatic illustration to date of the fallacy of the Responsibility of Peoples. . . . For-

tunately for the honor of science, a number of scientists refused to take part in the development of The Bomb. . . . They reacted as whole men, not as specialists or partisans. Today the tendency is to think of peoples as responsible and individuals as irresponsible. The reversal of both these conceptions is the first condition of escaping the present decline to barbarism. The more each individual thinks and behaves as a whole man (hence responsibly) rather than as a specialized part of some nation or profession (hence irresponsibly) the better hope for the future.[170]

During the Nürnberg War Crimes Trials following World War II the "Allies" declared in unmistakable language that the individual citizen is responsible for his actions regardless of what a government may require of him. The demand for unconditional obedience to one's government is no justification for doing wrong. This suggests that there are times when men see it as the duty of a citizen to act independently and to refuse to cooperate with his government.

If no firm objection is raised to oppose the diabolical use of government tax money in creating untold suffering for millions of innocent Vietnamese, are we not "guilty of an unchristian worship of the god of war"?[171]

Christian faithfulness involves having only one primary loyalty. When the empire or the nation asks to be put first, the Christian must thereby give an account of himself, explaining why he cannot conform fully. In this testimony there is always implied a criticism of the state's practice. The Christian who refuses to participate in idolatry speaks at first only for himself; but in reality he challenges implicitly the state's right to force its subjects to religious conformity. By refusing to perform military service he testifies against all war, even though he does not expect . . . that the state will disarm.[172]

By the same logic it could be said that by refusing to pay war taxes the Christian testifies against all war including the conscription of money which makes it possible. In this way, "prophetic tax refusal is not a denial of responsibility for the social situation, but acceptance of it in a personal encounter with evil and an attempt to deal redemptively with it."[173]

The true self-image of the churches and the correct definition of their proper role in the world is to be found in God's self-giving as revealed in Jesus.

The Christian churches need but turn to their own history to see such a value orientation in operation: their Founder was Himself a citizen of an occupied nation, and the Caesar whose image was on the coin was the foreign oppressor. In such a context the "give unto Caesar" instruction, which has since been elaborated into a blanket order to obey any national call to arms, could more convincingly be interpreted as a call to resistance (to nonviolent resistance when other scriptural texts are taken into account) to those demands of Caesar which go beyond his rightful due. This is the interpretation which seems to have prevailed throughout the catacomb era of Christian history, a period in which the goods of personal and national survival — and political freedom as well — were nowhere near as ultimate as they have come to be in the thinking of the majority of Christians who now seem prepared to accept virtually any extremes of violence to preserve them.[174]

If protest is incidental to the proclamation of the gospel then we should be grateful for the opportunity to demonstrate our desire to be good citizens, helpful members of society, and to show a reconciling spirit. However, the evidence seen above may suggest that our usual cooperation with the United States government and the IRS as the best expression of our Christian love and service is no longer immediately obvious. The assumption that Christians can support and obey all that our government demands should be critically and continually examined. There are times when individuals cannot and should not give obedience to government without examining the morality of the demand. Gordon Zahn holds that wherever there is a serious discrepancy between the moral order and the established political order, ". . . the moral obligation must always take precedence over the political or civic duty. . . . Individual Christians, either in response to . . . guidance or to the enlightenment offered by their own consciences, should refuse to take part voluntarily in any acts which do not pass the test of their moral criteria: . . ."[175] Consequently, we must sharpen the discrimination which separates the things which belong to God and the things which belong to Caesar. Where do we find the line between a direct contribution to war and an incidental assistance to war? Someone has said that it is not within the prerogatives of Christian obedience to exercise forms of power which cripple or smash the structures of the society, but it definitely is our business to use those forms and techniques of influence which so effectively expose the exaggerated claims of "the powers."

Can we delude ourselves any longer into opposing war without an equally vigorous opposition to the payment of war taxes? Edgar Metzler startled Christians when he wrote:

> In the day when land armies were crucial, conscientious objection had some significance. In today's world of technological warfare, it hardly matters.[176]

If his observation is correct, as it may well be, then it clearly points up the fact that we have allowed conscientious objection to war to become meaningless by default. Somehow we have failed to adequately relate the gospel to the changed and changing situation in today's world. If conscientious objection to war is to have any genuine significance in our time it must include a decisive "no" to the Internal Revenue Service for money which is clearly spent for war purposes. This step would extend the scope of noncooperation from mere refusal to serve in war to the nonpayment of war taxes. Unless this is done, we object to war with our bodies, but finance it through the money which we earn through our labor. What we need is to become conscientious objectors to war in *both* body and property. Frank H. Epp demonstrated a good understanding of the implications of the present situation when he wrote:

> In the days when the state asked primarily for men to go to war, we were conscientious objectors. But now the primary tool of war is money. Can we still be conscientious objectors now?[177]

It would be interesting to know how many individuals in Mennonite congregations would qualify as authentic conscientious objectors if examined on the basis of the United States government position "which has through its courts held several times that any substantial contribution for war by an individual is legal proof that he is not a genuine objector to war."[178] Conscientious objection to war, obviously, is not a new thing, but the practical implications of such a position might well be. "New occasions teach new duties" and our times require that this very old word be radically reinterpreted and adapted to the new situation. A. J. Muste stated a great truth when he wrote:

> In this age of mechanization, regimentation, and authoritarianism perhaps nothing is more important than that the individual should again learn to disobey evil laws, learn the tremendous power of refusal, of saying no. . . . Even among pacifists there is often a tendency to minimize the importance or validity of this no-saying, of conscientious objection, of refusal to go along, of noncooperation. It is said to be "meagerly negative" perhaps. From the moral standpoint those who advance this objection need to be very certain that they are not in effect cooperating with the evil which they profess to condemn.[179]

In the present age of military technology conscientious objection to military service is becoming less and less meaningful. Our conscientious protest to military preparations will have to take new and different forms if it is to retain its vital significance. Certainly the one most accessible and crucial in our day is the protest which we can register against war taxes (income and excise) collected through the Internal Revenue Service.

Wendal Bull has pointed out that every voluntary tax remittance constitutes "an unquestionable voucher of the remitter's consent to the government's policies."[180] And John Howard Yoder has reminded us that:

> Whereas military service involves only young men, . . . themselves too young to be fully qualified to analyze the challenge placed before them, every individual or at least every family unit faces the moral issue of income tax in the full knowledge that well over half of these funds are used for the arms race and for the militarization of American

society. Thus the responsibility for nonconformist action is laid before every individual; this increases both the significance of the moral issue itself and the likelihood that consistent Christian action would have witness value.[181]

After all, there is good precedent in the New Testament for following conscience whether or not a government makes it legal to do so. Not to follow one's conscience also involves a risk: "Some people have stopped listening to their consciences, and their faith has been wrecked" (1 Timothy 1:19, Laubach translation).

If as Christians we really believe that "to acquiesce in the manufacture and use of these weapons is . . . a sin against God, a sin against our fellowman, a sin against generations yet unborn"; if we really believe ". . . that war is contrary to the will of God and incompatible with the precepts and example of our Lord, Jesus Christ,"[182] then let us have the sense and courage of our convictions to stop paying taxes voluntarily and willingly to governments which continue to make and use these instruments of destruction. It could well be that such a decision would help us to recover what it means to be a disciple of Jesus Christ in our time. At least we would have the unsurpassed privilege of sharing "his sufferings" (Philippians 3:10). Although acquiescence may be the easier way, noncooperation with evil is our moral duty.

It has been said that the great mistake of the sixteenth-century Anabaptists was to be several centuries ahead of their time on controversial issues such as the separation of church and state, religious freedom, believer's baptism, and the principle of nonparticipation in war. Why should Christians at that time have protested so vigorously against the practices of the existing church and state? Why should they have "rocked the boat" and challenged things as they were? Why should they have acted upon their beliefs and taken the consequences of those decisions when it would have been much easier for them to be "the quiet in the land"? Although many of the Christian concepts promoted by the Anabaptists have since been accepted by Protestantism at large, this was not true during the sixteenth century. Many of them paid for their witness, their negativism, with their lives. For them it was an expression of their radical obedience and commitment to God as revealed in Jesus Christ their Lord. Perhaps they knew that their negativism would have positive results. In any case, like the Christians in the early church they challenged their society where it was wrong. In doing this they not infrequently broke the laws of governments, and there can be no doubt that majority opinion at that time condemned them for doing so.

If the Anabaptists were biblically correct in refusing to participate in war in any form, then it appears that it would be proper for Christians in our day to carry out the logical implications of their position in the area of war taxes, even as some did during the sixteenth century. Unless we have the courage and determination to dissociate ourselves completely from both war and preparations for war we shall be lagging behind the times rather than being ahead of the times. Moreover, we shall be in great danger of being unfaithful to God. The crucial issue, then, is whether what we do measures up to the kind of discipleship which is required of those who claim Jesus Christ as Lord.

J. John Friesen asserts that our commitment to God in Christ

clearly means a life of nonconformity to the world. It means a willingness to be different — not for the sake of being different, but for the sake of Jesus Christ. Jesus was different, the Anabaptists were different. They had to suffer. It takes courage to live by this principle.[183]

A good way for Christians to effectively demonstrate both their objection to war and their objection to participation in it, is to unite in a witness against the payment of war taxes. Such radical obedience to God's claim upon our lives means that from the world's point of view Christians really are "fools for Christ's sake" (1 Corinthians 4:10a). But then ". . . being a fool for Christ's sake should not be an insurmountable obstacle in the eyes of the Christian."[184] However, it would seem that the refusal to pay war taxes serves as one important way by which we in our time are permitted to maintain our integrity as "sons of God" in the face of tyrannical brutalities. Perhaps Christians are not able to be relevant to the present Vietnam crisis as the "world" thinks of relevancy. After all, Jesus' death on the cross did not appear to be very relevant to those who first witnessed the event. Fortunately, Jesus understood that His witness before God was far more important than His reputation before men. The Apostle Paul is confident that "God chose what is foolish in the world to shame the wise" (1 Corinthians 1:27a).

Admittedly, the right of taxation, including the gathering of taxes for war, has a long-established precedent in the history of governments. Despite this fact, is it not conceivable that even this "collective necessity" needs to be subject to the lordship of Christ? Throughout man's history there is abundant evidence that the collective is man's "all too frequent plea to justify wrong."[185] It happened at Jesus' crucifixion. It happens in our day whenever we justify an evil act in the interests of any group; whenever the collective will of a community becomes an absolute in itself, "overriding even the moral obligations inherent in its own heritage."[186]

> We blame the churches for failing to bear bold witness against war. It is true that they have sheltered themselves within church walls, set the cross on an altar and offered it symbolic homage. But what of us who have accepted the Christian injunction with all of its implications — to love our enemies and overcome evil with good — what are we doing about it, we who are too old to go to prison for refusing to kill? This tax money for bombs — this is not Caesar's. It is God's — the price of the lifeblood of our young men and all the young men of our human brotherhood. Are we not morally bound to hold back this money?[187]

How long will Christians "pray for peace" and continue to "pay for war"? The answer depends upon you. Every individual has the choice of paying or not paying for that which threatens all. Can those who really object to war ever pay others, including governments, to do what they themselves can not in good conscience do? If we are to be "Christian" in practice as well as by profession it is imperative that we promptly stop our voluntary participation in "killing via the tax method." God help us to throw off our timidity, and with courage, joy, and boldness to act more meaningfully.

In the words of Maurice F. McCrackin:

This evil chain of violence and death must be broken and it will be broken when enough individuals say to the state, "You may order me to do something I believe wrong, but I will not execute your command. You may order me to kill, but I will not kill nor will I give my money to buy weapons that others may do so." There are other voices that I must obey. I must obey the voice of humanity which cries for peace and relief from the intolerable burden of armaments and conscription. I must obey the voice of conscience, made sensitive by the inner light of truth. I must obey the voice heard across the centuries, "Love your enemies, . . . pray for them which despitefully use you, and persecute you." In obedience to these voices lies the only path to brotherhood and peace. And these are the voices I must obey.[188]

" 'Coinage' — For Whose Altar?"

Render unto Caesar —
It bears his image,
Buys missiles, napalm,
And the Bomb.
Trains the apple-cheeked marine
In gunnery and the bayonet.
And thus we preserve the
Image of God in man.

Render unto God —
"The earth is the Lord's and the fulness
thereof, the world and those who dwell therein."
Thine the Vietnamese madonna
Seared by jellied gasoline.
Thine the death-stopped marine
With cheek now fading.
Thine the incinerated Vietcong
And defoliated earth.
And thus we preserve the
Image of God in man?

What blasphemy is this?
We render unto Caesar that which is not his.
That which is not his![189]

Notes

1. J. A. Sanders, "Tax, Taxes," *Interpreter's Dictionary of the Bible*, Vol. 4 (New York: Abingdon Press, 1962), p. 520.

2. Isaac Mendelsohn, "Samuel's Denunciation of Kingship in the Light of the Akkadian Documents from Ugarit," *BASOR* No. 143 (October 1956), pp. 17-22.

3. Edward König, "Taxation," *Jewish Encyclopedia*, Vol. XII (New York: Funk and Wagnalls Company, 1912), p. 70.

4. Sanders, "Tribute," *op. cit.*, p. 710.

5. *Idem.*

6. König, *op. cit.*, p. 70.

7. Flavius Josephus, *Antiquities of the Jews* (Philadelphia, Pennsylvania: Henry T. Coates & Co.), Book XII, Chapter iv, Section 4 ff. Opinions differ as to the identity of this Hyrcanus with the grandson (?) of Tobias, John Hyrcanus I (134-104 BC), whose birth and history are related at considerable length by Josephus, or with another of the same name, John Hyrcanus II (78-69 BC and 63-40 BC), mentioned in *Antiquities of the Jews*, XIII, viii, 4.

8. B. J. Bamberger, "Tax Collector," *Interpreter's Dictionary of the Bible*, Vol. 4 (New York: Abingdon Press, 1962), p. 522.

9. Frederick C. Grant, *The Economic Background of the Gospels* (London: Oxford Univ. Press, 1926), pp. 36 f.

10. *Ibid.*, pp. 69, 70.

11. *Ibid.*, pp. 39, 40.

12. *Ibid.*, p. 47.

13. Sanders, "Tax, Taxes," *op. cit.*, p. 521.

14. S. Vernon McCasland, "New Testament Times: I. The Greco-Roman World," *The Interpreter's Bible*, Vol. 7 (New York: Abingdon Press, 1951), p. 96.

15. *Idem.*

16. Grant, *op. cit.*, p. 9.

17. *Ibid.*, p. 91.

18. *Ibid.*, p. 45.

19. *Ibid.*, p. 105.

20. *Ibid.*, p. 97.

21. *Ibid.*, p. 91.

22. *Ibid.*, p. 89.

23. *Ibid.*, p. 105.

24. *Ibid.*, p. 11.

25. *Ibid.*, p. 100.

26. *Ibid.*, p. 87.

27. Martin Rist, "Caesar or God (Mark 12:13-17)? A Study in Formgeschichte," *The Journal of Religion*, Vol. XVI (1936), p. 319.

28. Ethelbert Stauffer, *Christ and the Caesars* (Philadelphia: Westminster Press, 1955), p. 117.

29. A. C. Bouquet, *Everyday Life in New Testament Times* (New York: Charles Scribner's Sons, 1953), p. 16.

30. Grant, *op. cit.*, pp. 105 f.

31. Harold S. Bender, "Taxation," *Mennonite Encyclopedia*, Vol. IV (Scottdale, Pennsylvania: Mennonite Publishing House, 1959), pp. 687 f.

32. *Encyclopedia Britannica*, Vol. 21 (Chicago: Encyclopedia Britannica, Inc., 1956), p. 837.

33. Nancy E. Sartin, "Large Race in Small Arms," *The Mennonite*, Vol. 83:19 (May 7, 1968), p. 333.

34. C. Northcote Parkinson, *The Law and the Profits* (Boston: Houghton Mifflin Company, 1960), p. 38.

35. *Ibid.*, p. 42.

36. Hugh Montefiore, "Jesus and the Temple Tax," *New Testament Studies*, Vol. 11, No. 1 (October 1964), pp. 70, 71.

37. J. Duncan M. Derrett, "Peter's Penny: Fresh Light on Matthew 17:24-27," *Novum Testamentum*, Vol. VI, Fasc. I (Januari 1963), p. 14.

38. Montefiore, *op. cit.*, p. 65.

39. *Idem.*

40. Letter from Arthur Harvey (Canterbury, New Hampshire) dated June 24, 1968, p. 1.

41. *Ibid.*

42. Frederick C. Grant, *The Interpreter's Bible*, Vol. 7 (New York: Abingdon Press, 1962), p. 841.

43. Ernest R. Bromley, "Did Jesus Pay Taxes to Warring States?" *The Peacemaker* (November 21, 1959).

44. Oscar Cullmann, *The State in the New Testament* (New York: Charles Scribner's Sons, 1956), p. 36.

45. *Ibid.*, p. 37.

46. William Reuben Farmer, *Maccabees, Zealots, and Josephus* (New York: Columbia University Press, 1965), p. 200.

47. J. Spencer Kennard, Jr., *Render to God* (New York: Oxford University Press, 1950), p. 116.

48. Oscar Cullmann, *op. cit.*, p. 18.

49. Grant, *op. cit.*, p. 12.

50. *Ibid.*, p. 135.

51. *Ibid.*, p. 102.

52. Kennard, *op. cit.*, p. 118.

53. *Idem.*

54. *Ibid.*, p. 122.

55. *Ibid.*, p. 125.

56. *Ibid.*, p. 126.

57. *Ibid.*, pp. 104 f.

58. *Ibid.*, p. 137.

59. *Ibid.*, p. 139.

60. *Handbook on Nonpayment of War Taxes* (Raymond, New Hampshire: Greenleaf Books, January, 1966), p. 9.

61. Culbert G. Rutenber, *The Dagger and the Cross* (New York: Fellowship Publications, 1953), pp. 80, 81.

62. Jean Lasserre, *War and the Gospel* (Scottdale, Pennsylvania: Herald Press, 1962), p. 92.

63. C. E. B. Cranfield, *A Commentary on Romans 12-13* (Edinburgh & London: Oliver and Boyd, 1965), p. 61.

64. Cranfield, *op. cit.*, p. ix.

65. *Idem.*

66. Peter Meinhold, *Caesar's or God's* (Minneapolis, Minnesota: Augsburg Publishing House, 1962), p. 18.

67. Clinton D. Morrison, *The Powers That Be* (London: SCM Press, Ltd., 1960), p. 64.

68. Cullmann, *op. cit.*, pp. 55, 56.

69. *Ibid.*, pp. 56, 57.

70. *Ibid.*, p. 65.

71. *Ibid.*, p. 51.

72. *Ibid.*, p. 91.

73. *Ibid.*, pp. 69, 70.

74. *Ibid.*, p. 79.

75. *Ibid.*, p. 84.

76. Herbert M. Gale, "Paul's View of the State," *Interpretation*, Vol. VI, No. 4 (October 1952), pp. 411-14.

77. John Howard Yoder, *The Christian Witness to the State* (Newton, Kansas: Faith and Life Press, 1964), p. 75. The distinction between subjection and unconditional obedience is carefully worked out in Else Kaehler, *Die Frau in den paulinischen Briefen* (Zurich, 1960) pp. 172-197.

78. Peter Meinhold, *op. cit.*, p. 17.

79. *Ibid.*, p. 20.

80. Morrison, *op. cit.*, p. 128.

81. Lasserre, *op. cit.*, p. 109.

82. John Howard Yoder, "The Things That Are Caesar's" (Part I), *Christian Living* (July 1960), p. 5.

83. Lasserre, *op. cit.*, p. 111.

84. *Ibid.*, pp. 112 f.

85. G. H. C. MacGregor, "Principalities and Powers: The Cosmic Background of Paul's Thought," *New Testament Studies*, Vol. I, No. 1 (September 1954), p. 25.

86. Rist, *op. cit.*, p. 327.

87. Cranfield, *op. cit.*, pp. 79, 80.

88. *Ibid.*, p. 80.

89. Archie Penner, *The Christian, The State, and the New Testament* (Scottdale, Pennsylvania: Herald Press, 1959), p. 122.

90. Wilhelm Mensching, *Conscience* (Wallingford, Pennsylvania: Pendle Hill Pamphlets, 1961), p. 24.

91. This point of view is challenged by those who hold that conscientious objection is not in the draft law as a constitutional right related to the first amendment but has been deemed a privilege rather than a right.

92. Edward Gottlieb, Eulogy for Norman Mattoon Thomas, *War Resisters League News* (January-February 1969), p. 5.

93. Alfred Hassler, *Diary of a Self-Made Convict* (Nyack, New York: Fellowship Publications, 1958), p. 97.

94. Ralph Borsodi, *The Challenge of Asia* (Melbourne, Florida: Melbourne University Press, 1956), p. 51.

95. C. Henry Smith, *Christian Peace: Four Hundred Years of Mennonite Peace Principles and Practice.* (———: Peace Committee of the General Conference of the Mennonite Church of North America, 1938), p. 21.

96. Albert Luthuli, *Let My People Go* (New York: McGraw-Hill Book Company, Inc., 1962), p. 136.

97. Dwight Y. King, "General Hershey Versus the Holy Spirit," *Arena* (April 1968), A-2.

98. Milo Kauffman, *The Challenge of Christian Stewardship* (Scottdale, Pennsylvania: Herald Press, 1955), pp. 46, 47.

99. Milton Mayer, "Rendered unto Caesar," *Fellowship* (September 1, 1962), p. 14.

100. Frank H. Epp, "On the Topic of the Tax," *The Mennonite* (March 7, 1961), p. 151.

101. J. R. Burkholder, "Radical Pacifism Challenges the Mennonite Church" (paper prepared for the Mennonite Theological Study Group, January 1960), p. 2.

102. King, *op. cit.*, A-3.

103. Borsodi, *op. cit.*, p. 160.

104. James Russell Lowell, "War" (poem), *Christian Living* (July 1969), inside front cover.

105. John E. Steen, "Death and Taxes" leaflet (204 1/2 W. Third St., Santa Ana, California: Orange County Peace and Human Rights Center, 1969).

106. Hans A. De Boer, *The Bridge Is Love* (London: Marshall, Morgan and Scott, 1957), p. 255.

107. Kennard, Jr., *op. cit.*, p. ix.

108. *Ibid.*, p. 123.

109. *Ibid.*, p. 124.

110. Faith and Life Press bulletin No. 6691 (Newton, Kansas: Faith and Life Press).

111. Elizabeth Hershberger Bauman, *Coals of Fire* (Scottdale, Pennsylvania, Herald Press, 1954), p. 37.

112. William Klassen, "We Must Obey and Pay, But We May Also Protest: A Study of Taxes and the New Testament," *The Canadian Mennonite* (April 19, 1963), p. 5.

113. James C. Juhnke, "Youth & Taxes," *The Mennonite* (April 24, 1962), p. 286.

114. Lowell, *op. cit.*, inside front cover.

115. Daniel Zehr, "Mennonites and War Taxes" (an article submitted to the Peace Section, Mennonite Central Committee, Akron, Pennsylvania, on February 21, 1968), p. 1.

116. Roy Pearson, "War, Taxes, Stewardship," *The Mennonite* (March 1, 1960), p. 143.

117. John M. Swomley, Jr., *The Military Establishment* (Boston: Beacon Press, 1964), p. 112.

118. Charles A. Wells, *Journey into Light* (Princeton, New Jersey: Between the Lines Press, 1958), pp. 89, 90.

119. Parkinson, *op. cit.*, p. 126.

120. Lasserre, *op. cit.*, p. 184.

121. C. Henry Smith, *The Story of the Mennonites* (Newton, Kansas: Mennonite Publication Office, 1957), p. 150.

122. Franklin Hamlin Littell, *The Anabaptist View of the Church* (Boston: Starr King Press, 1958), p. 90.

123. *Ibid.*, p. 105.

124. George Huntston Williams, *The Radical Reformation* (Philadelphia, Pennsylvania: Westminster Press, 1962), p. 225.

125. *Mennonite Encyclopedia*, Vol. II, p. 848.

126. G. R. Elton (ed.). *The New Cambridge Modern History*, Vol. II, *The Reformation 1520-1559* (Cambridge: Cambridge University Press, 1958), p. 123.

127. Williams, *op. cit.*, p. 225.

128. Harold S. Bender, "Taxation," *Mennonite Encyclopedia*, Vol. IV, p. 688.

129. Williams, *op. cit.*, p. 231.

130. Anson Phelps Stokes, *Church and State in the United States*, Vol. I (New York: Harper & Bros., 1950), pp. 112 f.

131. Williams, *op. cit.*, p. 748.

132. Ernest R. Bromley, "The Case for Tax Refusal," *Fellowship* (November 1947), p. 172.

133. Franklin Zahn (compiler), "Historical Notes on Conscience Vs. War Taxes" (836 So. Hamilton Blvd., Pomona, California), p. 1.

134. Guy F. Hershberger, *Nonresistance and the State* (Scottdale, Pennsylvania), Mennonite Publishing House, 1937), p. 33.

135. Janet Whitney (ed.). *The Journal of John Woolman* (Chicago: Henry Regnery Company, 1950), pp. 66, 68.

136. Franklin Zahn, *op. cit.*, p. 3.

137. Stokes, *op. cit.*, p. 757.

138. William Warren Sweet, *The Story of Religion in America* (New York: Harper & Bros., 1950), p. 187.

139. *Ibid.*, p. 186.

140. Harold S. Bender, "Kleine Gemeinde," *Mennonite Encyclopedia*, Vol. III, p. 196.

141. Stokes, *op. cit.*, p. 772.

142. Quoted by Wilbur Bender, *Nonresistance in Colonial Pennsylvania* (Scottdale, Pennsylvania: Mennonite Publishing House, 1934), p. 18.

143. Melvin Gingerich, *Service for Peace* (Akron, Pennsylvania: The Mennonite Central Committee, 1949), pp. 2, 3.

144. Gingerich, *op. cit.*, p. 3.

145. *Ibid.*, p. 4.

146. *Ibid.*, p. 5.

147. Richard B. Gregg, *The Power of Non-Violence* (New York: Fellowship Publications, 1951), p. 20.

148. Quoted in War Resisters League leaflet and the *Handbook on Nonpayment of War Taxes* (Raymond, New Hampshire: Greenleaf Books, Second Edition, January, 1966), p. 17.

149. Gordon Charles Zahn, *War, Conscience and Dissent* (New York: Hawthorn Books, Inc., 1967), pp. 272 f.

150. De Boer, *op. cit.*, p. 112.

151. Excerpt from *Tolstoy's Writings on Civil Disobedience and Non-Violence, Fellowship* (November 1967), p. 32.

152. P. Regamey, *Non-violence and the Christian Conscience* (London: Darton, Longman and Todd, 1966), pp. 214 f.

153. Quoted in a War Resisters League leaflet.

154. Dale Aukerman, *et al,* "A Call to Income Tax Protest," (1451 Dundee Ave., Elgin, Illinois: General Brotherhood Board, Church of the Brethren, November 25, 1960), p. 5.

155. "Baez Files Claim with IRS for Refund of 1965 Tax," *Fellowship Peace Information Edition* (October 1966), p. 2.

156. Second edition published January 1966 at Raymond, New Hampshire, by Greenleaf Books.

157. King, *op. cit.*, A-2.

158. John Howard Yoder, Memo to Peace Problems Committee on "Income Tax Refusal" (October 15, 1962), p. 4. .

159. *Ibid.*, p. 2.

160. M. A. C. Warren, *Caesar, the Beloved Enemy* (Chicago: Alec R. Allenson, Inc., 1955), p. 94.

161. Arthur Harvey (ed.), *Theory and Practice of Civil Disobedience* (Raymond, New Hampshire: Arthur Harvey, 1961), p. 8.

162. Sartin, *op. cit.*, p. 334.

163. Ted Webster (compiler), *War Tax Resistance: Individual Witness or Community Movement* (45 Winthrop Street, Roxbury, Massachusetts: Roxbury War Tax Scholarship Fund, 1968), p. 9.

164. Erwin N. Hiebert, *The Impact of Atomic Energy* (Newton, Kansas: Faith and Life Press, 1961), p. 287.

165. *Idem.*

166. *Ibid.*, p. 271.

167. *Ibid.*, p. 270.

168. Chapel talk at Goshen Biblical Seminary on February 7, 1968.

169. King, *op. cit.*, A-4.

170. Dwight Macdonald, *The Root Is Man* (Alhambra, California: The Cunningham Press, 1953), p. 55.

171. De Boer, *op. cit.*, p. 207.

172. Yoder, "The Things That Are Caesar's," *op. cit.*, p. 5.

173. Melvin D. Schmidt, "Tax Refusal as a Form of Conscientious Objection to War," a study prepared at the Divinity School, Yale University (1964), p. 11.

174. Gordon Zahn, *An Alternative to War* (New York: The Council on Religion and International Affairs, 1963), pp. 24-5.

175. Gordon Charles Zahn, *op. cit.*, p. 118.

176. Edgar Metzler, Editorial, *The Mennonite*, 78:14 (April 2, 1963), p. 239.

177. Epp. *op. cit.*, p. 151.

178. Source of quotation unknown.

179. A. J. Muste, *Not by Might* (New York: Harper & Bros., 1947), p. 150.

180. *Handbook on Nonpayment of War Taxes* (Raymond, New Hampshire: Greenleaf Books, February 1963), p. 5.

181. Yoder, *op. cit.*, p. 2.

182. Hiebert, *op. cit.*, p. 272.

183. J. John Friesen, *What Does It Mean to Be a Mennonite?* (North Newton, Kansas: Mennonite Press, 1964), p. 13.

184. Gordon Charles Zahn, *op. cit.*, p. 294.

185. M. Kamel Hussein, *City of Wrong, A Friday in Jerusalem* (Amsterdam: N. V. Djambatan, 1959), p. xiv.

186. *Ibid.*, p. xv.

187. Caroline Urie (1874-1955, a colleague of Jane Addams), *Handbook on Nonpayment of War Taxes*, p. 5. Also in leaflet, "Why We Refuse to Pay Taxes for War" (August 1956).

188. Arthur and Lila Weinberg (editors). *Instead of Violence* (Boston Beacon Press, 1963), p. 90.

189. Jim Harnish, poem, "Coinage," is accompanied by a drawing of a hand holding a coin with the caption, "For Whose Altar?" *The Mennonite* (Feb. 20, 1968), p. A-5 of *Central District Reporter*.

Bibliography

Books and Pamphlets

"A Proposed Bill" — the "Civilian Income Tax Act of 1961" as drawn up by the Pacific Yearly Meeting of Friends, Claremont, Calif.

Allen, E. L. *Pacifism as an Individual Duty*. London: 1946.

Aukerman, Dale *et al*. "A Call to Income Tax Protest." 1451 Dundee Ave., Elgin, Ill.: General Brotherhood Board, Church of the Brethren (November 1960). 4 pages plus appendix.

Bainton, Roland H. *Christian Attitudes Toward War and Peace*. (A Historical Survey and Critical Re-evaluation). New York: Abingdon Press, 1960.

————. *Early Christianity*. Princeton, N.J.: D. Van Nostrand Co., Inc., 1960.

Bargen, Bennie. "My Income Tax Pilgrimage" (May 6, 1960). North Newton, Kan. (included in Leo Driedger's 6-page compilation).

Barnet, Richard J. *The Economy of Death*. 1969.

Barr, Stringfellow. *Citizens of the World*. Garden City, N.Y.: Doubleday & Company, Inc., 1953.

Bauman, Elizabeth Hershberger. *Coals of Fire*. Scottdale, Pa.: Herald Press, 1954.

Beaver, R. Pierce. *Envoys of Peace* (The Peace Witness in the Christian World Mission). Grand Rapids, Mich.: Eerdmans, 1964.

Bender, Ross T. *The People of God: A Mennonite Interpretation of the Free Church Tradition*. Scottdale, Pa.: Herald Press, 1971.

Bender, Wilbur. *Nonresistance in Colonial Pennsylvania*. Scottdale, Pa.: Mennonite Publishing House, 1934.

Berkhof, H. (translated by John Howard Yoder). *Christ and the Powers*. Scottdale, Pa.: Herald Press, 1962.

Bonhoeffer, Dietrich. *The Cost of Discipleship*. New York: Macmillan Co., 1956.

Borsodi, Ralph. *The Challenge of Asia*. Melbourne, Fla.: Melbourne Univ. Press, 1956.

Boulding, Kenneth E. *The Organizational Revolution* (A Study in the Ethics of Economic Organization). New York: Harper & Bros., 1953.

Bouquet, A. C. *Everyday Life in New Testament Times*. New York: Charles Scribner's Sons, 1953.

Bowman, Rufus D. *Seventy Times Seven*. Elgin, Ill.: Brethren Publishing House, 1945. (Esp. p. 122.)

Bright, John. *The Kingdom of God*. New York and Nashville: Abingdon Press, 1953.

Brock, Peter. *Pacifism in the United States from the Colonial Era to the First World War*. Princeton, N.J.: Princeton Univ. Press, 1968. (See "War Tax.")

Brown, Dale W. *Brethren and Pacifism*. Elgin, Ill.: The Brethren Press, 1970.

Burkholder, J. R. "Radical Pacifism Challenges the Mennonite Church" (paper prepared for the Mennonite Theological Study Group, January 1960), 16 pages.

Butterfield, Herbert. *Christianity and History*. London: Collins Press, 1949, 1957.

Buttrick, George Arthur (ed.). *The Interpreter's Bible* (12 volumes). New York: Abingdon Press, 1957.

————(ed.). *The Interpreter's Dictionary of the Bible* (4 volumes), New York: Abingdon Press, 1962.

Cadoux, Cecil John. *The Early Christian Attitude to War: A Contribution to the*

History of Christian Ethics. London: Headley Bros., 1919, 1940.
—————. *The Early Church and the World*. Edinburgh: T. & T. Clark, 1925.
Calvert, Robert, *Ain't Gonna Pay for War No More*. 339 Lafayette St., New York: War Tax Resistance, 1971. Revised, 1972.
Charles, Howard H. *God and His People*. Scottdale, Pa.: Herald Press, 1969.
Chodorov, Frank. *The Income Tax — Root of All Evil*. New York: Devin-Adair Company, 1954, 1963.
Church of the Brethren. "A Statement to Leaders of the United States Government" (A statement on poverty, racism, and war adopted by the Church of the Brethren Annual Conference, Ocean Grove, N.J., June 1968). 1451 Dundee Ave., Elgin, Ill.: Church of the Brethren General Offices.
—————. "Statement of the Church of the Brethren on War." (As Revised by the Church of the Brethren Annual Conference, Ocean Grove, N.J., June 1968). 1451 Dundee Ave., Elgin, Ill.: Church of the Brethren General Offices.
—————. "Taxes for War Purposes." (A Statement Adopted by the Brethren Service Commission, General Brotherhood Board, November 1967). 1451 Dundee Ave., Elgin, Ill.: Church of the Brethren General Offices.
Chute, Marchette. *Jesus of Israel*. New York: E. P. Dutton & Co., Inc., 1961.
Clergy and Laymen Concerned About Vietnam. *In the Name of America*. New York: Clergy and Layman Concerned About Vietnam, 1968.
Cook, Fred J. *The Warfare State*. New York: The Macmillan Company, 1962.
"Counsel About War Tax Payment" and "Approaches and Method of Tax Objection." (Two statements prepared in 1968 by the Peace and Social Concerns Committee, Board of Christian Service, 722 Main Street, Newton, Kan. 67114.
Cousins, Norman. *In Place of Folly*. New York: Harper & Bros., 1961.
Cranfield, C. E. B. *A Commentary on Romans* 12-13 (Scottish Journal of Theology Occasional Papers, No. 12). Edinburgh: Oliver and Boyd, 1965.
Cullmann, Oscar. *The State in the New Testament*. New York: Charles Scribner's Sons, 1956.
De Boer, Hans A. *The Bridge Is Love*. London: Marshall, Morgan & Scott, 1957.
Derleth, August. *Concord Rebel, A Life of Henry D. Thoreau.* . . Chilton Books, 1962.
Detweiler, Richard C. *Mennonite Statements on Peace 1915-1966*. Scottdale, Pa.: Herald Press, 1968.
Dimont, Max I. *Jews, God and History*. New York: The American Library of World Literature, Inc., 1962.
Douglass, James W. *The Nonviolent Cross*. New York: Macmillan Company, 1968.
Driedger, Leo. "Positions on Tax Dollars for War Purposes," a 6-page compilation in mimeographed form. Newton, Kan.: General Conference Mennonite Church, Board of Christian Service, 1960.
—————. "Acceptable and Non-acceptable Forms of Witness" (A Special Study Report). 600 Shaftesbury Boulevard, Winnipeg 29, Man., Canada: Canadian Board of Christian Service.
Durant, Will. *The Story of Civilization III: Caesar and Christ*. New York: Simon Schuster, 1944.
Dyck, Cornelius J. (ed.). *An Introduction to Mennonite History*. Scottdale, Pa.: Herald Press, 1967.
Ekirch, Arthur A., Jr. *The Civilian and the Military*. New York: Oxford Press, 1956.
Elton, G. R. (ed.). *The New Cambridge Modern History: The Reformation 1520-1559*, Vol. 2, Cambridge: Cambridge Univ. Press, 1958.
Encyclopedia Americana (30 volumes). New York: Americana Corporation, 1954.

Encyclopaedia Britannica (24 volumes). Chicago: Encyclopaedia Britannica,Inc., 1956.

Enz, Jacob J. *The Christian and Warfare: The Roots of Pacifism in the Old Testament.* Scottdale, Pa.: Herald Press, 1972.

Epp, Frank H. *Mennonite Exodus* (The Rescue and Resettlement of the Russian Mennonites Since the Communist Revolution). Altona, Man.: D. W. Friesen & Sons, Ltd., 1962.

Farmer, William Reuben. *Maccabees, Zealots, and Josephus* (An Inquiry into Jewish Nationalism in the Greco-Roman Period). New York: Columbia Univ. Press, 1956.

Fast, Henry A. *Jesus and Human Conflict.* Scottdale, Pa.: Herald Press, 1959.

Ferguson, John. *The Enthronement of Love.* London: Fellowship of Reconciliation, 1950.

Friesen, Gerhard. "My Story on Income Taxes" (June 10, 1960). Newton, Kan. (included in Leo Driedger's 6-page compilation).

Friesen, J. John. *What Does It Mean to Be a Mennonite?* North Newton, Kan.: Mennonite Press, 1964.

General Conference Mennonite Church. "A Christian Declaration on Peace, War and Military Service" (adopted at Portland, Ore., Aug. 22, 1953), 11 pages. 722 Main St., Newton, Kan. 67114. Board of Christian Service, General Conference Mennonite Church.

————. *The Way of Peace* (a 1971 position statement). Available from Commission on Home Ministries, 722 Main St., Box 347, Newton, Kan., 67114.

Gibbon, Edward. *The Decline and Fall of the Roman Empire.* New York, Dutton.

Gingerich, Melvin. *Service for Peace.* Akron, Pa.: The Mennonite Central Committee, 1949.

Gish, Arthur G. *The New Left and Christian Radicalism.* Grand Rapids, Mich.: William B. Eerdmans Publishing Co., 1970.

Gottfried, Sue. *What Do You Mean — Nonviolence?* (The Story of Wars Without Weapons.) Nyack, N.Y.: Fellowship Publications.

Gottwald, Norman K. *All the Kingdoms of the Earth* (Israelite Prophecy and International Relations in the Ancient Near East). New York: Harper & Row, 1964.

Graber, Ralph. "Evaluation of the McCrackin Case as Related to Radical Pacifism" (A Research Paper). Elkhart, Ind.: Mennonite Biblical Seminary, January 1961.

Grant, Bruce. *Indonesia.* London and New York: Cambridge Univ. Press, 1964.

Grant, Frederick C. *The Economic Background of the Gospels.* London: Oxford Univ. Press, 1926.

Green, Mrs. Edith. *A Bill H. R. 12310* (To establish a people's program for peace, to provide for investments in peace through the United Nations, to permit deductions from personal income taxes for payments made thereto, and for other purposes), May 1, 1958.

————. *Joint Resolution, J. J. Res. 253* (To provide a credit against the individual income tax for individuals who make contributions or gifts to the United Nations or its specialized agencies), February 18, 1963.

Gregg, Richard B. *The Power of Non-Violence.* New York: Fellowship Publications, 1951.

Gregory, Dick (edited by James R. McGraw). *The Shadow That Scares Me.* New York: Doubleday and Company, Inc., 1968.

Habegger, David L. "Interpreting Matthew 22:17-22" (a mimeographed study consisting of two pages), 1968, Elkhart, Ind.

Handbook for War Tax Resistance. 339 Lafayette St., New York: War Tax Resistance, September 1970. 14 pp.

Handbook on Nonpayment of War Taxes. Raymond, New Hampshire: Greenleaf

Books, Arthur Harvey for the Peacemaker Movement, Cincinnati, Ohio, February 1963. Second edition published January 1966.

"Hang up on War!" — Telephone War Tax Refusal Campaign (leaflet). 5 Beekman Street, Room 1025, New York, N.Y.: War Resisters League.

Harding, Walter. *A Thoreau Handbook*. New York: New York University Press, 1959.

Hartzler, J. S. *Mennonites in the World War, or Nonresistance Under Test*. Scottdale, Pa.: Mennonite Publishing House, 1921.

Harvey, Arthur. *Theory and Practice of Civil Disobedience*. Raymond, N.H.: Arthur Harvey, 1961.

Heering, Gerrit Jan. *The Fall of Christianity: A Study of Christianity, The State and War*. London: G. Allen and Unwin, 1930 (or New York: Fellowship Publications, 1943).

Hellerstein, Jerome R. *Taxes, Loopholes and Morals*. New York: McGraw-Hill, 1963.

Hennacy, Ammon. *The Book of Ammon*. Salt Lake City, Utah: Published by the author, 1965.

Hershberger, Guy Franklin. *Nonresistance and the State*. (The Pennsylvania Quaker Experiment in Politics 1682-1756). Scottdale, Pa.: Mennonite Publishing House, 1936.

—————. *The Mennonite Church in the Second World War*. Scottdale, Pa.: Mennonite Publishing House, 1951.

—————. (ed.). *The Recovery of the Anabaptist Vision*. Scottdale, Pa.: Herald Press, 1957 (See page 190).

—————. *War, Peace, and Nonresistance*. Scottdale, Pa.: Herald Press, 1953.

Hiebert, Erwin N. *The Impact of Atomic Energy*. Newton, Kan.: Faith and Life Press, 1961.

Hunter, Allan A. *Christians in the Arena*. New York: Fellowship, 1958.

—————. *Courage in Both Hands*. New York: Ballantine Books, Inc., 1962.

Hussein, M. Kamel. *City of Wrong. A Friday in Jerusalem*. Amsterdam: N. V. Djambatan, 1959 (or Seabury paperback, New York).

Hutchinson, Paul. *The New Leviathan*. Chicago: Willett, Clark & Co., 1946.

Jackson, Samuel Macauley (ed). *Schaff-Herzog Encyclopedia of Religious Knowledge* (13 volumes). New York: Funk & Wagnalls Co., 1911.

Johnsen, Julia Emily (compiler). *Conscription of Wealth in Time of War*. New York: H. H. Wilson Co., 1930.

Johnson, Sherman E. *Jesus in His Homeland*. New York: Charles Scribner's Sons, 1957. Especially pages 87-128.

Jones, Rufus M. (ed.). *The Church, The Gospel and War*. New York: Harper & Bros., 1948.

Josephus, Flavius. *Antiquities of the Jews and Wars of the Jews*. Philadelphia, Pa.: Henry T. Coates & Co.

Kauffman, Milo. *The Challenge of Christian Stewardship*. Scottdale, Pa.: Herald Press, 1955.

Kaufman, Don and Eleanor. Letter to "Commissioner of Internal Revenue, and . . . Secretary for Tax Legislation" dated March 30, 1960 (also included in Leo Driedger's 6-page compilation).

Kaufman, Ed. G. "The Christian and Nuclear Warfare," an article prepared for the Seventh Mennonite World Conference held in Kitchener, Ont., during August 1962, and which is included in *The Lordship of Christ* edited by Cornelius J. Dyck (1962), pp. 536-44.

Kee, Howard Clark, and Franklin W. Young. *Understanding the New Testament*. Englewood Cliffs, N.J.: Prentice-Hall, Inc., 1957.

Kennard, J. Spencer, Jr. *Render to God* (A Study of the Tribute Passage). New York: Oxford Univ. Press, 1950.

King, Martin Luther, Jr. *Stride Toward Freedom: The Montgomery Story*. New York: Harpers, 1958.

King, Rachel H. *God's Boycott of Sin*. New York: Fellowship Publications, 1946.

Kohn, Hans. *Nationalism, Its Meaning and History*. Princeton: D. Van Nostrand, 1955.

Krehbiel, Henry P. *War, Peace, Amity*. Newton, Kan.: H. P. Krehbiel, 1937.

Larson, Martin M. *The Great Tax Fraud*. New York: The Devin-Adair Co.

Lasserre, Jean. *War and the Gospel*. Scottdale, Pa.: Herald Press, 1962.

Latourette, Kenneth Scott. *A History of Christianity*. New York: Harper & Bros., 1953.

"Legal Avoidance of Taxes for War," 339 Lafayette St., New York: War Tax Resistance, 1970. 7 pages.

Leiper, Henry Smith. *The Ghost of Caesar Walks* (The Conflict of Nationalism and World Christianity). New York: Friendship Press, 1935.

Lens, Sidney. *The Counterfeit Revolution*. Boston: The Beacon Press, 1952.

Lindsay, ————. *A Bill H. R. 2144* (To amend the Internal Revenue Code of 1954 so as to permit charitable contributions, bequests, transfers, and gifts to the United Nations International Children's Emergency Fund (UNICEF) to be deductible for income tax, estate tax, and gift tax purposes), January 17, 1963.

Littell, Franklin Hamlin. *From State Church to Pluralism*. New York: Doubleday & Co., 1962.

————. *The Anabaptist View of the Church*. Boston: Star King Press, 1958.

Lonsdale, Kathleen. *Is Peace Possible?* Baltimore, Md.: Penguin Books, Inc., 1957.

Luthuli, Albert. *Let My People Go*. New York: McGraw-Hill Book Co., Inc., 1962.

Lynd, Staughton (ed.). *Nonviolence in America: A Documentary History*. New York: Bobbs-Merrill Co., Inc., 1966.

Macdonald, Dwight. *The Root Is Man*. Alhambra, Calif: The Cunningham Press, 1953.

Macgregor, G. H. C. *The New Testament Basis of Pacifism & the Relevance of an Impossible Ideal*. Nyack, N.Y.: Fellowship Publications, 1960.

————. "What Does the New Testament Say?" *New Age for Peace* (Fellowship of Reconciliation, 29 Great James Street, London, W.C.I.).

Martin, James J. *Men Against the State*. DeKalb, Ill.: Adrian Allen Association, 1953.

Mast, Russell. *A Basis for Christian Pacifism* (sermon). Newton, Kan.: Faith and Life Press.

Mayer, Milton. *On Liberty: Man Versus the State* (with a Center discussion). Santa Barbara, Calif.: The Center for the Study of Democratic Institutions, December 1969.

Mayer, Peter (ed.). *The Pacifist Conscience*. New York: Holt, Rinehart & Winston, 1966.

McGrath, William R. *Why We Are Conscientious Objectors to War*. Mission Home, Va.: Published by the author.

McNeer, May, and Lynd Ward. *Armed with Courage*. New York: Abingdon Press, 1957.

MCC WORKBOOK Reports and Statistics for 1959 (Annual Meeting Jan. 22, 23, 1960). Akron, Pa.: Mennonite Central Committee, 1960. Page B-8.

MCC WORKBOOK Reports and Statistics for 1960 (Annual Meeting Jan. 20, 21, 1961). Akron, Pa.: Mennonite Central Committee, 1961. Page B-6 "Income

Tax'' (Peace Section).

Means, Paul Banwell. *Things That Are Caesar's: The Genesis of the German Church Conflict.* New York: Round Table Press, 1935.

Meinhold, Peter. *Caesar's or God's?* (The conflict of church and state in modern society.) Minneapolis, Minn.: Augsburg Publishing House, 1962.

Meltzer, Milton and Walter Harding. *A Thoreau Profile.* New York: Thomas Y. Crowell Company, 1962.

Menninger, Karl. *Man Against Himself.* New York: Harcourt, Brace & Company, 1938.

Mennonite Central Committee Annual Report 1960 (Peace Section). Akron, Pa.: Mennonite Central Committee.

Mennonite Encyclopedia (4 volumes). Scottdale, Pa.: Mennonite Publishing House. 1955-59.

Mensching, Wilhelm. *Conscience.* Wallingford, Pa.: Pendle Hill Pamphlets, 1961.

Merton, Thomas, *et al. Breakthrough to Peace:* Twelve Views on the Threat of Thermonuclear Extermination. New York: New Directions, 1962.

──────. *Faith and Violence* (Christian Teaching and Christian Practice). Notre Dame, Ind.: University of Notre Dame Press, 1968.

Miller, William Robert. *Nonviolence: A Christian Interpretation.* New York: Association Press, 1964.

Mills, C. Wright. *The Causes of World War Three.* New York: Simon and Schuster, 1958. See especially chapter 21, published as "A Pagan Sermon" in *Christian Living* magazine, April 1960, pp. 16-18.

Minnesota Clergy and Laymen Concerned. *Churches and Phone Tax Resistance.* 122 West Franklin Ave., Minneapolis, Minn.: Kay Halverson & Carole Nelson, 1972.

Moellering, Ralph Luther. *Modern War and the American Churches.* New York: American Press, 1956.

Moore, George Foot. *Judaism* (Vol. II). Cambridge, Mass.: Harvard Univ. Press, 1932, pp. 70-73.

Morrison, Clinton D. *The Powers That Be: Earthly Rulers and Demonic Powers in Romans 13:1-7.* London: SCM Press Ltd., 1960.

Muste, A. J. *Not by Might.* New York: Harper & Bros. Publishers, 1947.

──────. *Of Holy Disobedience.* Wallingford, Pa.: Pendle Hill Publications, 1952.

Neufeld, Elmer, and John Unruh. Report of "Discussion at Annual Peace Section Meeting, Chicago, Ill., Jan. 21, 1960. Query: 'Can the nonresistant Christian in good conscience pay war taxes?' " 5 pages.

New Catholic Encyclopedia (15 volumes). New York: McGraw-Hill Book Co., 1967.

Niemoeller, Martin. *God Is My Fuehrer.* New York: Philosophical Library and Alliance Book Corporation, 1941.

Nock, Albert Jay. *Our Enemy, The State.* Caldwell, Idaho: The Caxton Printers, Ltd., 1959.

Nuttall, Geoffrey. *Christian Pacifism in History.* 1730 Grove St., Berkeley, Calif.: World Without War Council.

Nygren, Anders. *Commentary on Romans.* Philadelphia: Muhlenberg Press, 1949.

Parkinson, C. Northcote. *The Law and the Profits.* Boston: Houghton Mifflin Company, 1960.

Pascal, Blaise. *Pensees.* New York: E. P. Dutton and Company, Inc., 1960.

Pauling, Linus Carl. *No More War.* New York: Dodd, Mead, and Co., 1958.

Peachey, Paul (ed.). *Biblical Realism Confronts the Nation.* Nyack, N.Y.: Fellowship Publications, 1963.

Penner, Archie. *The Christian, The State, and the New Testament.* Scottdale, Pa.: Herald Press, 1959.

Phelps, Wm. L. *Christ or Caesar: The Religion of Jesus and the Religion of Nationalism.* New York: E. P. Dutton & Co., 1930.

Pike, James A. *Doing the Truth.* Garden City, N.Y.: Doubleday & Co., Inc., 1955.

Poling, David. *The Last Years of the Church.*

Puidoux Theological Conference, 1st Report "The Lordship of Christ over Church and State," 1955 (2nd edition, April 1960). Available from Peace Section, MCC, Akron, Pa.

Quanbeck, Warren A. (ed.). *God & Caesar* (A Christian Approach to Social Ethics). Minneapolis, Minn.: Augsburg Publishing House, 1959.

"Refuse to Pay War Taxes" (leaflet). New York: War Resisters League, Tax Resistance Project, 1969.

Regamey, P. *Non-violence and the Christian Conscience.* London: Darton, Longman and Todd, 1966.

Ricoeur, Paul. *The State and Coercion.* Geneva, Switzerland: John Knox House, 1957.

Rolston, Holmes. *The Social Message of the Apostle Paul.* Richmond Va.: John Knox Press, 1942.

Rutenber, Culbert G. *The Dagger and the Cross* (An Examination of Christian Pacifism). New York: Fellowship Publications, 1950.

————. *"The Totalitarian State and the Individual Conscience."* Nyack, N.Y.: Fellowship of Reconciliation.

Scherer, Paul. *The Christian Faith and Modern War.* New York: Church Peace Mission, 195—.

Schmidt, Melvin D. "Income Tax Refusal as a Method of Civil Disobedience," a social ethics paper presented to the Divinity School, Yale University (Dr. Liston Pope). New Haven, Conn. (June 5, 1964).

————. "Tax Refusal as a Form of Conscientious Objection to War," a study prepared at the Divinity School, Yale University (Dr. Gustafson), New Haven, Conn. (1964).

Schnackenburg, Rudolf. *The Moral Teaching of the New Testament.* London: Burns and Oates, 1965.

Schrag, Dale R. "Anabaptism: A Search for a Usable Past," a research paper presented to the Department of History, Bethel College (Dr. Keith Sprunger), North Newton, Kan. (May 1969).

Sibley, Mulford Q. (ed.). *The Quiet Battle: Writings on the Theory and Practice of Non-Violent Resistance.* Garden City, N.Y.: Anchor Books, 1963.

Singer, Isidore (ed.). *The Jewish Encyclopedia* (12 volumes). New York: Funk & Wagnalls Company, 1912.

Smith, C. Henry. *Christian Peace: Four Hundred Years of Mennonite Peace Principles and Practice. . . .* Peace Committee of the General Conference of the Mennonite Church of North America, 1938.

————. *The Story of the Mennonites.* Newton, Kan. Mennonite Publication Office, 1957.

Solberg, Richard W. *God and Caesar in East Germany.* New York: Macmillan, 1961.

Soper, Donald O. *Popular Fallacies About the Christian Faith.* London: The Epworth Press, 1938, 1957.

Speak Truth to Power, A Quaker Search for an Alternative to Violence. Philadelphia, Pa.: American Friends Service Committee, 1961.

Stauffer, Ethelbert. *Christ and the Caesars* (Historical Sketches). Philadelphia: Westminster Press, 1955.

110

Steen, John E. "Death and Taxes" (leaflet). 204 1/2 W. 3rd St., Santa Ana, Calif.: Orange County Peace and Human Rights Center, 1969.

Stokes, Anson Phelps. *Church & State in the United States* (3 volumes). New York: Harper & Bros., 1950.

Swalm, E. J. (compiler). *Nonresistance Under Test* (A Compilation of Experiences of Conscientious Objectors as Encountered in Two World Wars). Nappanee, Ind.: E. V. Publishing House, 1949.

Sweet, William Warren. *The Story of Religion in America*. New York: Harper & Bros., 1950.

Swomley, John M., Jr., *American Empire* (The Political Ethics of Twentieth-Century Conquest). London: The Macmillan Company, Collier-Macmillan Ltd., 1970.

————. *The Military Establishment*. Boston: Beacon Press, 1964.

Thoreau, Henry David. *Walden and Civil Disobedience* (a Norton Critical Edition with texts, background, and reviews). Edited by Owen Thomas. New York: W. W. Norton and Company, 1966.

————. *Walden* and *On the Duty of Civil Disobedience*. New York: Collier Books, 1962.

Tittle, Ernest Fremont. *Christians in an Unchristian Society*. New York: Association Press, 1939.

Tolstoi, Leo. *The Kingdom of God and Peace Essays*. New York: Oxford Univ., 1936.

Tussman, Joseph (ed.). *The Supreme Court on Church and State*. New York: Oxford Univ. Press, 1962.

Unruh, John D. *In the Name of Christ* (A History of MCC 1920-51). Scottdale, Pa.: Herald Press, 1952.

Van Braght, Thieleman J. *The Bloody Theater or Martyrs Mirror of the Defenseless Christians*. Scottdale, Pa.: Mennonite Publishing House, 1951.

Warren, M. A. C. *Caesar, the Beloved Enemy* (Three Studies in the Relation of Church & State). Chicago: Alec R. Allenson, Inc., 1955.

Webster, Ted (compiler). *War Tax Resistance: Individual Witness or Community Movement*. 45 Winthrop Street, Roxbury, Mass.: Roxbury War Tax Scholarship Fund, 1968.

Wieand, David J. (ed.). *The Church, Today and Tomorrow*. (The Bethany Faculty Series, No. 1.) Elgin, Ill.: Brethren Publishing House, 1947. Esp. pp. 36 ff.

Weinberg, Arthur & Lila (eds.). *Instead of Violence*. Boston: Beacon Press, 1963.

Wells, Charles A. *Journey into Light*. Princeton, N. J.: Between the Lines Press, 1958.

Wenger, J. C. *Pacifism and Biblical Nonresistance* (Focal pamphlet No. 15). Scottdale, Pa.: Herald Press, 1968.

Whitney, Janet (ed.). *The Journal of John Woolman*. Chicago: Henry Regnery Co., 1950.

Williams, George Huntston. *The Radical Reformation*. Philadelphia: Westminster Press, 1962.

Willcox, Walter Ross Baumes. *The Curse of Modern Taxation*. New York: Fortuny's, 1938.

Willoughby, William, *et al. 6 Papers on Peace* (A Symposium). 1451 Dundee Ave., Elgin, Ill.: Church of the Brethren General Offices, 1969.

Wilson, E. Raymond, Frances E. Neely, & Constance Longshore. *The Big Hand in Your Pocket*. 160 North 15th St., Philadelphia 2, Pa.: Peace Education Program, American Friends Service Committee, August 1960.

Wilson, Edmund. *The Cold War and the Income Tax: A Protest*. New York: Farrar, Straus, & Co. 1963.

Wood, James E., Jr. *The Problem of Nationalism in Church-State Relationships.* (Focal pamphlet No. 18). Scottdale, Pa.: Herald Press, 1968.

World Book Encyclopedia (20 volumes). Chicago: Field Enterprises Educational Corporation, 1964.

Wright, Edward Needles. *Conscientious Objectors in the Civil War.* Philadelphia: Univ. of Pa. Press, 1931.

Yoder, John Howard. Memo to Peace Problems Committee (General Conference of the Mennonite Church) on the "Subject: Income Tax Refusal" (Oct. 15, 1962), 4 pages.

————. *Nevertheless, A Meditation on the Varieties and Shortcomings of Religious Pacifism.* Scottdale, Pa.: Herald Press, 1971.

————. *Peace Without Eschatology?* Zeist, The Netherlands: Heerewegen Conference, 1954. Also a CONCERN reprint, 1961.

————. *The Christian Witness to the State.* Newton, Kan.: Faith & Life Press, 1964.

————. *The Original Revolution* (Essays on Christian Pacifism). Scottdale, Pa.: Herald Press, 1972.

Zahn, Franklin. "Alternative Service for Tax Dollars" (Distributed by Claremont Friends Meeting, c/o 836 S. Hamilton Blvd., Pomona, Calif.).

————(compiler). "Historical Notes on Conscience Vs. War Taxes," 836 S. Hamilton Blvd., Pomona, Calif. 5 pages.

————. Mimeographed letter "To Those Concerned About War Taxes" (New Year's Day, 1963).

————. "On the 'Civilian Income Tax Bill' " (Nov. 19, 1961).

Zahn, Gordon. *An Alternative to War.* New York: The Council on Religion & International Affairs, 1963.

————. *In Solitary Witness: The Life & Death of Franz Jagerstatter.* New York: Holt, Rinehart & Winston, 1964.

————. *War, Conscience and Dissent.* New York: Hawthorn, 1967.

Zehr, Daniel. "Mennonites and War Taxes," (An article submitted to the Peace Section, Mennonite Central Committee, Akron, Pa., on Feb. 21, 1968), 3 pages.

Periodicals

"Ammon's Tax Associates: COs Against War (Taxes)," *The Reporter for Conscience' Sake* (December 1971, p. 3.

"An Alternative to the payment of . . . income taxes earmarked for defense," *MCC News and Notes* (Dec. 31, 1959), p. 3.

"An Urgent Message to Our Churches from the 1967 Council of Boards" (adopted Dec. 1), *The Mennonite* (Dec. 12, 1967), pp. 753 f.

"Arvada Church Refuses to Pay Phone Tax for War," *The Mennonite* (Dec. 7, 1971), p. 732.

Baez, Joan C. Handwritten letter to IRS, *Time* (Apr. 17, 1964), p. 52.

————. "My Country Has Gone Mad . . . I Will Not Go Mad with It," *The Peacemaker*, Vol. 18, No. 7 (May 8, 1965), p. 1.

————. "Noted Singer Refuses to Pay Taxes That Go for War Preparation," *The Peacemaker*, Vol. 17, No. 6 (Apr. 18, 1964), p. 1.

Bainton, Roland C. "McCrackin Before the Assembly," *The Christian Century* (Apr. 18, 1962), pp. 488-90.

"Baptists May Withhold Excise Tax," *The Christian Leader* (Jan. 11, 1972), p. 18.

Baresch, Ruby. "Constructive Participation" (letter to the editor), *The Mennonite* (Mar. 17, 1964), p. 172.

Barnes, Peter. "Withholding War Taxes," *The New Republic* (Apr. 10, 1971).

Bass, Henry. Review of Milton Mayer's *On Liberty: Man Vs the State*, *Win* magazine, (May 1, 1970), pp. 24-26.

Bender, Harold S. "Church and State in Mennonite History," *Mennonite Quarterly Review*, Vol. XIII, No. 2 (Apr. 1939), pp. 83-103.

————. "When May Christians Disobey the Government?" *Gospel Herald*, Vol. LIII, No. 2 (Jan. 12, 1960), pp. 25, 26 and 44.

Bernhardt, Virgie. "McCrackin's Conscience and the Church," *Fellowship*, Vol. 27, No. 1 (Jan. 1, 1961), pp. 21-24.

————. "The McCrackin Verdict," *The Christian Century* (July 5, 1961), pp. 826-28.

Blackaby, Frank. "History's Greatest Dead End," *Saturday Review* (Mar. 14, 1970), pp. 19-21, 46.

Bollinger, Russell V. *et al.* "On Paying War Taxes: Four Alternatives," *Messenger* (Church of the Brethren) (Sept. 26, 1968), pp. 2-7.

Borchert, Wolfgang (translated and copyrighted by Elmer Suderman). "Say No! Sag Nein!" (poem), *Mennonite Life* (July 1971), pp. 105, 126, 142, 143, & inside back cover.

Borntrager, Elmer. "As I See It" (an exposition of Matthew 22:21), *Gospel Herald* (Apr. 13, 1971), p. 333.

Bowman, John G. "It's Not Enough to Pray That Your Money Go for Bridges," *With* (October 1971), pp. 20-23.

Breen, Quirinus. Book review of Ethelbert Stauffer's *Christ and the Caesars*, *Encounter*, Vol. 17, No. 3 (Summer, 1956), pp. 290-92.

"Brethren District Protests Phone Tax," *The Reporter for Conscience' Sake* (December 1971), p. 3.

"Brethren Give up Holdings in War-Related Companies," *The Mennonite* (Apr. 18, 1972), p. 269.

Brockington, L. H. Book Review of *Render unto Caesar* by Herbert Loewe, *Journal of Theological Studies*, Vol. 42 (1941), pp. 211 f.

Bromley, Ernest R. "Did Jesus Pay Taxes to Warring States?" *The Peacemaker* (Nov. 21, 1959).

————. "Is Tax Refusal Effective?" *Fellowship*, Vol. XIII, No. 11 (December 1947), pp. 189 f.

————. "Jesus and the Tax Question," *Zions Herald* (Mar. 10, 1948).

————. "The Army Draft and the Money Draft," *The Peacemaker* (Mar. 12, 1956).

————. "The Case for Tax Refusal," *Fellowship*, Vol. XIII, No. 10 (November 1947), pp. 171-73.

————. "The Taxpayer's Role as the Modern Soldier," *The Peacemaker* (Mar. 5, 1960).

————. "We Go to the Tax Man Empty-Handed," *The Peacemaker* (Apr. 28, 1962), p. 1.

Bromley, Marion. "'Alternative Service' for War Tax Dollars?" *The Peacemaker* (Feb. 18, 1961), pp. 3 f.

Brown, Robert McAfee. "The Berrigans: Signs or Models?" *Holy Cross Quarterly*, Vol. 4, No. 1 (January 1971), pp. 40-48.

Brueggemann, Walter A. "God's Word in Our World: Revolting Taxes and the Taxpayers' Revolt," *United Church Herald*.

Brunk, Harry A. "Virginia Mennonites and the Civil War," *Christian Living* (July 1961), pp. 14-17.

Burkholder, James, *et al.* "The Church in the Secular State," *Builder* (November 1972), pp. 21-30.

Casey, William Van Etten (ed.). "Thank You, Dan and Phil" (editorial), *Holy Cross Quarterly*, Vol. 4, No. 1 (January 1971), p. 3.

Charles, Howard H. "The Troublesome Tax Question," *Builder* (November 1972), pp. 19, 20, 30.

Chomsky, Noam. "On the Limits of Civil Disobedience," *Holy Cross Quarterly*, Vol. 4, No. 1 (January 1971), pp. 22-31.

"Church: Agent or Victim of Change?" *Messenger*, Church of the Brethren (Aug. 3, 1967), esp. p. 8.

"Cincinnati Presbytery Deposes McCrackin," *Fellowship Peace Information Edition* (Apr. 15, 1963), p. 4.

Clifford, Richard J. "The Berrigans: Prophetic?" *Holy Cross Quarterly*, Vol. 4, No. 1 (January 1971), pp. 14, 16, 18.

"Conscientious Objection During the Civil War," *The Reporter for Conscience' Sake* (June 1962), 2, 4, 5, and 6.

Coppock, David. "Taxes for War Purposes" (letter to the editor), *Messenger* (Church of the Brethren), (Jan. 30, 1969), inside front cover.

"Court Rules Out Conscience on Income Tax," *The Reporter for Conscience' Sake*, Vol. XVIII, No. 3 (March 1961), p. 4.

Cranfield, C. E. B. "Some Observations on Romans XIII, 1-7." *New Testament Studies*, Vol. VI (1959-60), pp. 241-49.

Cratchit, Bob. "How to Cheat on Your Income Tax: A Guide," *Ramparts* (April 1972), pp. 32, 33, 36-38.

Curran, C. E. "Taxation & Moral Obligation," *New Catholic Encyclopedia*, Vol. 13 (1967) pp. 950 f.

Deckert, Marion. "Most of all concerned" — a letter to the editor. *The Mennonite* 83:23 (June 4, 1968), p. 396.

"'Demonstrate Biblical Citizenship' — A resolution on nationalism with proposals for study and action adopted by the General Conference Mennonite Church at Estes Park, Colo., on July 18." *The Mennonite*, 83:32 (Sept. 10, 1968), p. 566.

Dellums, Ronald V. "World Peace Tax Fund Act," H.R. 14414, *Congressional Record* (Apr. 17, 1972). 4 legal-size pages.

Denney, J. "Caesar and God," *The Expositor*, 5th series, Vol. 3 (1896), pp. 61-69.

Derrett, J. Duncan M. "Peter's Penny: Fresh Light on Matthew XVII, 24-27," *Novum Testamentum*, Vol. VI, Fasc. 1 (January 1963). (Also see review in *New Testament Abstracts*, Vol. 8, No. 3 (Spring, 1964), p. 351.

Dickinson, Robert E. "Why I Cannot Pay War Taxes" (letter), *The Peacemaker* (Feb. 26, 1972), p. 1.

Dods, Marcus. "The Stater in the Fish's Mouth," *The Expositor*, Series 3, Vol. 7 (1888), pp. 461-72.

Drescher, John. "Dare We Pay Taxes for War?" *Gospel Herald* (Oct. 10, 1967), p. 909.

————. "Taxes for War" (editorial), *Gospel Herald* (June 27, 1972), p. 545.

Driedger, Leo. "Alternative to Income Tax," *Report*, Vol. III, No. 3, (Autumn, 1960), Akron, Pa.: Mennonite Central Committee, p. 18.

————. "Questions Asked at Conference," *The Mennonite* (Nov. 13, 1962), p. 726.

————. "The Taxes That Go to War," *The Mennonite* (Jan. 15, 1963), pp. 38 f.

Duff, Edward. "The Burden of the Berrigans," *Holy Cross Quarterly*, Vol. 4,

No. 1 (January 1971), pp. 4-12.

"Eastern Seminars Discuss Response to War Taxes," *The Mennonite* (Apr. 18, 1972), p. 269.

Ediger, Peter. "An American Trilogy" (poem), *The Mennonite* (May 16, 1972), p. 336.

Enns, John F. "A Christian's Dilemma" — an open letter to IRS and their reply, *The Mennonite* (May 10, 1960), p. 307.

Epp, Frank H. "On the Topic of the Tax" (Focus on Christian Concerns), *The Mennonite* (Mar. 7, 1961), p. 151.

Erb, Paul. "Focus on World Issues at Lansdale Session," *Mennonite Weekly Review* (Aug. 31, 1967), p. 6.

Esbensen, Steve. "Brethren Draft Statement on War Taxes," *The Reporter for Conscience' Sake* (March 1969), p. 3.

Fawcett, Colin. "Should a Pacifist Refuse Income Tax?" *Reconciliation*, XI (December 1959), pp. 227-29.

Fleming, D. F. "The End of the World Before the End of the Century?" *Katallagete. Be Reconciled* (Fall, 1970), pp. 27-30.

FOR Executive Committee. "The Spock et al Case: A Statement," *Fellowship* (March 1968), p. 8.

Franz, Delton. "Your Tax Dollars at Work," *Washington Memo*, MCC Peace Section (November-December 1971), pp. 1, 2.

Franz, Robert A. "Extra Deductions on Benevolent Giving," *The Mennonite* (Dec. 24, 1963), p. 778.

Freeman, Miles C. "Declines to Pay Income Tax" (letter), *The Greenleaf* (June 14, 1963), pp. 3 f.

Friedman, Michael. "Why Do Mennonites Buy War? or Why Mennonites Pray for Peace and Pay for War?" *The Mennonite Draft Resistance Newsletter* (February 1972), pp. 2, 5.

Friesen, Jane. "Commitment on Tax Issue" (letter to the editor), *The Mennonite* (May 4, 1971), p. 302.

Gale, Herbert M. "Paul's View of the State" (A Discussion of the Problem in Romans 13:1-7), *Interpretation*, Vol. 6 (October 1952), pp. 409-14.

Gallo, O. K. "No Such Thing as a War Tax" (letter to the editor), *The Mennonite* (Apr. 27, 1971), p. 284.

Gingerich, Melvin. "Perplexing Question Raised: 'What Belongs to Caesar?' " (book review), *Mennonite Weekly Review* (May 11, 1972).

Goering, Jack. "Biblical Issues Raised by War Tax Workshop," *The Mennonite* (Mar. 23, 1971), pp. 190, 191.

Goertzen, Ardean L., *et al.* "Should Christians Pay War Taxes?" (statement adopted by the Western District on Oct. 24, 1970), *The Mennonite* (Nov. 10, 1970), pp. 682, 683.

Goppelt, L. "The Freedom to Pay the Imperial Tax (Mark 12:17)," *Studia Evangelica*, ed. by F. L. Cross, Vol. II, pp. 183-94.

Gottlieb, Edward. Eulogy for Norman Mattoon Thomas, *War Resisters League News* (January-February 1969), p. 5.

Graber, Steve. "Force or Nonresistance," *The Northern Light* (March 1967), pp. 4, 7, 8.

Grant, W. J. "Citizenship and Civil Disobedience" (Romans XIII), *Expository Times*, Vol. 54 (April 1943), pp. 180 f.

Greeley, Andrew M. "The Berrigans: Phrenetic?" *Holy Cross Quarterly*, Vol. 4, No. 1 (January 1971), pp. 15, 17, 19.

Guth, Robert W. "War Taxes in 1777" (letter to the editor), *The Mennonite* (Nov. 28, 1972), p. 704.

Habegger, David L. "Shall We Pay War Taxes?" *The Mennonite* (Mar. 14, 1972), pp. 182, 183.

Hackman, Walt. "Not Size of the Group but Strength of Vision!" *Gospel Herald* (Dec. 12, 1972), pp. 1017, 1018.

Hall, Cameron P. "Paying Taxes: A Christian Obligation," *Social Action*, Vol. 27, No. 2 (October 1960), pp. 13-21.

Hall, Clarence W. "The Revolt of the 'Plain People,' " *Reader's Digest* (November 1962), pp. 74-78.

Harnish, Jim. " 'Coinage' — For Whose Altar?" *The Mennonite* (Feb. 20, 1968), p. A-5 of Central District Reporter.

Haselden, Kyle. "God and the Lure of This Life's Caesars," *The Pulpit*, Vol. XXXII, No. 8 (August 1961), pp. 3 and 19.

Helstern, Russell. "I Confess I Am Deeply Troubled" — an open letter to the editor. *Messenger*, Church of the Brethren, Vol. 116, No. 7 (Mar. 30, 1967), p. 26.

Hennacy, Ammon. "A Pinch of Incense," *Fellowship* (June 1950).

Hertzler, Daniel. "Death and Taxes" (editorial), *Christian Living* (April 1970), p. 40.

Hertzler, Joseph. "Saying No to War Taxes," *Peace News* (Bethel College, Kan.) (Oct. 15, 1970), pp. 5, 6.

Hillerbrand, Hans J. "The Anabaptist View of the State," *Mennonite Quarterly Review*, Vol. XXXII, No. 2 (April 1958), pp. 83-110.

Hilty, Judy. "Protests Are a Way to Speak," *The Mennonite* (May 2, 1961), pp. 298 f.

Hilty, Minerva. "Work to Make Things Right" (letter to the editor), *The Mennonite* (Jan. 12, 1971), p. 30.

Hood, Daniel E. "Emperor's Suit Looks Good" (letter to the editor), *The Mennonite* (June 8, 1971), p. 385.

Hooley, Alvin. "Readers Say," *Gospel Herald* (Aug. 1, 1972), p. 618.

Horst, Samuel L. "Our Readers Say — ," *Gospel Herald* (Apr. 9, 1963), p. 292.

Hostetter, Doug. "American Youth Visit Vietnamese People," *The Mennonite* (Feb. 2, 1971), pp. 68, 69.

Janzen, David. "Das Neue Buch, 'What Belongs to Caesar?' " *Der Bote* (Feb. 22, 1972).

—————. "Pay to Tax Conscience Fund" (a statement submitted as a letter to *The New York Times* but not accepted for publication), *The Mennonite* (Apr. 6, 1971), pp. 236, 237.

Janzen, Lois Barrett. "Mennonites and Participation in Politics," *The Mennonite* (Nov. 7, 1972), pp. 648, 649.

—————. "War Tax Resisters Rally Twice in Spite of IRS," *VS Newsletter* (June 1972), p. 2.

Jezer, Martin. "Tax Refusal," *WIN Peace & Freedom Through Nonviolent Action*, Vol. 3, No. 6 (Mar. 24, 1967), p. 9.

Juhnke, James, *et al.*, "Christian Witness Against the Military Tax" (a tax refusal letter), *Peace Section Newsletter*, Vol. 1, No. 2 (Apr. 25, 1970), pp. 5, 6.

—————. "Our Almost Unused Political Power," *The Mennonite* (Oct. 10, 1967), pp. 606 f.

—————. "Mennonites and the Great Compromise," *The Mennonite*, 83:34 (Sept. 23, 1969), pp. 562-64.

—————. "Youth and Taxes," *The Mennonite*, Vol. 77, No. 17 (Apr. 24, 1962), pp. 285 f.

Kallas, J. "Romans XIII, 1-7: An Interpolation," *New Testament Studies*, Vol. 11, No. 4 (July 1965), pp. 365-74.

Kaufman, Don. "Paying for War" (letter to the editor), *The Mennonite* (Feb. 18, 1964), p. 108.

———. "The Readers Write," *Mountain Lake Observer* (Apr. 8, 1971), pp. 2, 7.

———. "War Taxes, Should They Be Paid?" (Chapter 8), *Program Guide 1971 for Sunday Evening Services*, Arnold C. Roth, editor, pp. 38-42.

Kaufman, Don and Eleanor. Letter to Internal Revenue Service, Washington 25, D.C., *The Mennonite* (June 9, 1959), p. 359.

Keeney, William. "Dutch Mennonites Discuss Problems of the Nuclear Era," MCC *News Service Release* (Apr. 30, 1963), 4 pages.

Kehler, Larry. "After the Calm" (editorial), *The Mennonite* (Apr. 18, 1972), p. 275.

Kepler, Mr. and Mrs. Roy C. "Letter to a Tax Collector," *Fellowship* (April 1957), pp. 14, 15.

King, Dwight Y. "General Hershey Versus the Holy Spirit," *Arena* (Student edition of *The Mennonite*, April 1968), pp. A-2-A-4.

Klassen, Donald R. "A Protest on War Taxes" (letter to the editor), *The Mennonite* (July 1, 1969), p. 444.

Klassen, Peter James. "Bibliographical and Research Notes on 'The Economics of Anabaptism, 1525-1960,'" *Mennonite Quarterly Review* (April 1963), pp. 131, 132.

Klassen, William. "Coals of Fire: Sign of Repentance or Revenge?" *New Testament Studies*, Vol. 9 (1963), pp. 337-50.

———. "Jesus and the Ten Commandments," *Adult Bible Study Guide*, Vol. XXVI, No. 1 (January-March, 1962). North Newton, Kan.: Board of Education and Publication of the General Conference Mennonite Church, pp. 72, 73, and 75.

———. "Protestants Seek to Understand Role of Church and State," *The Mennonite* (Mar. 10, 1964), pp. 150-152, or "The Relation of the Church and the State," *The Canadian Mennonite* (Mar. 3, 1964), p. 6.

———. "We Must Obey and Pay, But We May Also Protest: A Study of Taxes and the New Testament," *The Canadian Mennonite* (Apr. 19, 1963), p. 5.

Kniss, Lloy A. "Our Readers Say — ," *Gospel Herald* (Mar. 19, 1963), pp. 228 and 244.

Kreider, Carl. "The Church in Chains" — Book Review of Richard W. Solberg's *God and Caesar in East Germany*, *Christian Living* (August 1962), p. 32.

Kroeker, Dave. Book Review of "*What Belongs to Caesar?* A Discussion on the Christian's Response to Payment of War Taxes, by Donald D. Kaufman," *The Mennonite Quarterly Review*, Vol. 46, No. 1 (January 1972), pp. 91, 92.

Kuhn, J. W. "Tax Surcharge: Paying for the War," *Christian Century*, Vol. 27 (Nov. 13, 1967), pp. 257, 258.

Lapp, John A. "Church Institutions and the Collection of Taxes (War) — a Query" (a brief memorandum addressed to the MCC Peace Section to stimulate thought and debate).

Lefever, Donald R. "An Open Letter to the President," *Messenger*, Church of the Brethren, Vol. 115, No. 11 (May 26, 1966), inside cover page.

Lehman, Carl M. "Tax Refusal Is Effective" (letter to the editor), *The Mennonite* (June 29, 1971), p. 432.

———. "Tax Refusal Not Politically Effective" (letter to the editor), *The Mennonite* (June 1, 1971), pp. 368, 369.

Liberty, Stephen. "Pharisees, Herodians, and 'just men, as the Questioners about the Tribute," *Expository Times*, Vol. 28, (August 1917), pp. 522 f.

Liechty, Daniel. "Reexamination Needed" (letter to the editor), *The Mennonite* (Nov. 28, 1972), p. 705.

Lind, Millard. "Freedom and Education" — an editorial on the First Amendment to the Constitution of the U.S.A., *Christian Living* (September 1958), p. 2.

Livingston, Richard A. "The Night Thoreau Spent in Jail," *Messenger* (Apr. 15, 1971), pp. 28, 29.

Loewen, Esko. "Church and State," *Mennonite Life*, Vol. XI, No. 3 (July 1956), pp. 141 f.

Love, Kennett. "Tax Resistance — An Alternative to Violence," *The Washington Monthly* (December 1969), pp. 60-65.

Lowell, James Russell. "War" (poem). *Christian Living* (July 1969), inside front cover.

Macgregor, G. H. C. "Principalities and Powers: The Cosmic Background of Paul's Thought," *New Testament Studies*, Vol. 1, No. 1 (September 1954), pp. 17-28.

Malishchak, Richard. "Some Thoughts on Peace Taxes," *Gospel Herald* (Oct. 31, 1972), pp. 885, 886.

Mark, Leslie E. "Caesar's Rights," *HIS* (November 1955), pp. 23-25.

Mayer, Milton. "April 15: If You Want Mylai, Buy It," *The Progressive* (April 1971), pp. 20-23.

————. "Mr. Wilson's Wars," *Liberation* (December 1963), p. 26.

————. "The Things That Are Not Caesar's," *Fellowship* (February 1948).

————. "Rendered unto Caesar," *Fellowship* (Sept. 1, 1962), pp. 11-16, and 32-34.

"Mayer's Tax Suit Dismissed," *News Notes* of the Central Committee for Conscientious Objectors (June 1957), p. 1.

"MCC Notes Increase in Tax-Refusal Donations," *The Mennonite* (May 9, 1972), p. 317.

"McCrackin and His Church" — Letters to the Editor, *The Christian Century* (Dec. 6, 1961), pp. 1468-70.

"McCrackin" — Letters to the Editor, *The Christian Century* (Aug. 16, 1961), p. 983.

McCrackin, Maurice. "Guns and Bombs — I Do Not Want to Buy Them," *The Peacemaker* (Vol. VII, No. 12 1/2, June 3, 1957), pp. 2, 3. (Tax Refusal Edition).

McKenney, John L. "A Time for Conscience," *Fellowship*, Vol. 35, No. 7 (July 1969), pp. 19-22.

Meehan, Mary. "What If They Gave a War and Nobody Paid?" *Fellowship* (Fall, 1971), pp. 13-15.

Mendelsohn, Isaac. "Samuel's Denunciation of Kingship in the Light of the Akkadian Documents from Ugarit," BASOR (Bulletin American Schools of Oriental Research), No. 143 (October 1956), pp. 17-22.

Metzler, Edgar. "Editorial," *The Mennonite*, 78:14 (Apr. 2, 1963), p. 239.

Meyer, Karl. "How to Beat the Withholding System (tax resistance beyond April 15)," *WIN Peace and Freedom Through Nonviolent Action*, Vol. IV, No. 16 (Sept. 16, 1968), pp. 14, 15.

Meyer, Ron. "Reflections on Paying War Taxes," *Gospel Herald* (May 23, 1972), pp. 465, 466.

Miller, Merlin G. "Alternative Service for Tax Dollars," *Messenger* (Church of the Brethren) (Aug. 28, 1969), p. 28.

"Minister Refuses to File Tax . . . Again," *The Christian Century* (May 17, 1960), p. 20.

118

Mittwoch, A. "Tribute and Land-Tax in Seleucid Judea," *Biblica*, Vol. 36, Fasc. 3 (1955), pp. 352-61.

Montefiore, Hugh. "Jesus and the Temple Tax," *New Testament Studies*, Vol. II, No. 1 (October 1964), pp. 60-71.

Moore, Richard E. "Airing Facts in the McCrackin Case," *The Christian Century* (Nov. 28, 1962), pp. 1447-49.

Moyer, A. M. "Our Readers Say — ," *Gospel Herald* (Mar. 26, 1963), pp. 252 and 261.

Mumford, Lewis. "The Morals of Extermination," *The Atlantic* (October 1959), pp. 38-44. Also an American Friends Service Committee reprint.

Murphy, Robert. "Tax Refusal Campaign," *WIN Peace & Freedom Through Non-violent Action*, Vol. 3, No. 8 (Apr. 28, 1967), p. 13.

Muste, A. J. "Why I Refuse to Pay Income Taxes — My Affair with the Internal Revenue Bureau," *Liberation* (April and May 1960), pp. 4, 17-19.

"Muste Loses Tax Case," *News Notes* (March-April 1961), pp. 1, 2.

Myers, David S. "Most of all foolish" (letter to the editor), *The Mennonite*, 83:16 (Apr. 16, 1968), p. 287.

Neufeld, Elmer, and John Unruh, "Ultimate Warning," *The Mennonite* (May 3, 1960), p. 284.

"News from the Peace Front" concerning Karel F. Botermans and Arthur Evans. *Fellowship Peace Information Edition* (May 1, 1963), p. 3. (Also issue of Sept. 1, 1963, p. 3.)

Nobile, Philip. "Phil Berrigan in Prison" (an untold story of Senator Goodell and Doctor Coles), *Holy Cross Quarterly*, Vol. 4, No. 1 (January 1971), pp. 32-35, 37, 38.

North, Karl. "IRS Tries to Seize Car for Phone Tax" (a letter on the moral and political implications of tax refusal), *The Peacemaker* (Sept. 7, 1968), p. 6.

"Obedience to God and Civil Disobedience" — a policy statement of the Church of the Brethren, *Messenger*. (May 22, 1969), pp. 22-25.

Obluda, Paul. "Why War Tax Resistance?" *WIN (Peace and Freedom Through Non-violent Action)*, (Apr. 15, 1971), pp. 10-16.

O'Brien, David J. "The Berrigans and America," *Holy Cross Quarterly*, Vol. 4, No. 1 (January 1971), pp. 52-58.

"Pacific Friends Push Alternative Tax Proposal," *Fellowship*, Vol. 27, No. 7 (Apr. 1, 1961), p. 1.

Pauls, Jacob and Irene. "Obey Conscience" (letter to the editor), *The Mennonite* (Sept. 5, 1972), p. 513.

"Paying War Taxes: Ought There Be an Alternative?" *Messenger* (Church of the Brethren), (Sept. 12, 1968), pp. 14, 15.

"Peace Assembly Considers Money, Military," *The Mennonite* (Dec. 5, 1972), p. 714.

Peacemaker leaflet, "The Imperative of Saying No to War Taxes," *The Peace-maker* (Jan. 16, 1971, issue as an insert).

"Peacemakers Plan Demonstrations in Washington on Tax Deadline," *The Peace-maker* (Apr. 1, 1961), p. 1

Peachey, J. Lorne. "No Money for War," *Christian Living* (January 1968), p. 11.

————. "To Heal the Scars of War," *Christian Living* (June 1968), p. 11.

Pearson, Roy. "War, Taxes . . . and Stewardship," *Pulpit Digest* (January 1960), p. 38. — Reprinted in *The Mennonite* (Mar. 1, 1960), p. 143.

Peters, Harold. "Warfare Versus Welfare" (letter to the editor), *The Mennonite* (Feb. 27, 1962), p. 139.

Piel, Gerard. "The Fork in the Road," *Harvard Alumni Bulletin* (July 7, 1962).

"Proposed: A World Peace Tax Fund," *The Reporter for Conscience' Sake* (December 1971), pp. 1, 3.

"Quakers Press Government for Employees' Tax Money," *The Mennonite* (July 28, 1970), pp. 479, 480.

Raines, John C. "The Followers of Life," *Holy Cross Quarterly*, Vol. 4, No. 1 (January 1971), pp. 65-69.

Ratzlaff, Keith. "On Being Scared" (The Page, N.D. Youth), *The Northern Light* (April 1972), p. 10.

————. "The Way Chose You," *The Mennonite* (Apr. 11, 1972), p. 260.

Regier, Austin. "Christianity and Conscription as Viewed by a Non-Registrant," *The Mennonite* (Nov. 30, 1948), pp. 13-15.

————. "The Faith of a Convict," *The Mennonite* (Feb. 15, 1949), pp. 8-10.

Regier, Raymond. "Taxes Are Part of War Effort" (letter to the editor), *The Mennonite* (June 29, 1971), p. 432.

Reimer, Richard. "Facing the Race," *The Mennonite* (Jan. 3, 1961), pp. 5, 6.

Rempel, Wendell. "Is Noncooperation a Responsible Christian Witness?" *The Mennonite* (May 19, 1970), pp. 338-342.

Rensberger, Lois. "The Case of David Rensberger, 22," *Christian Living* (September 1971), pp. 4-6.

Rist, Martin. "Caesar or God (Mark 12:13-17)? A Study in Form-geschichte," *Journal of Religion*, Vol. XVI, No. 3 (July 1936), pp. 317-31.

Roszak, Theodore. "Tax Delinquent and Dissenter," *Liberation* (December 1963), p. 27.

Royer, Howard E. "The Campaign to Hang Up on War," *Messenger*, Church of the Brethren, Vol. 116, No. 16 (Aug. 17, 1967), pp. 13, 14.

————. "Portraits of Asia," *Messenger*, (Feb. 15, 1971), pp. 6, 7, 30, 31.

Runnels, Jim. "War Tax Refusal," *Fellowship*, Vol. 33, No. 11 (November 1967), 13.

Sartin, Nancy E. "Large Race in Small Arms," *The Mennonite*, 83:19 (May 7, 1968), pp. 332-35.

Sawatzky, Mrs. Leroy L. "The Readers Write," *Mountain Lake Observer* (Apr. 22, 1971).

Sax, Joseph L. "Civil Disobedience: The Law Is Never Blind," *Saturday Review* (Sept. 28, 1968), pp. 22-25 and 56.

Schmidt, Melvin D. "Avoidance of Truth" (letter to the editor), *The Mennonite*, 83:23 (June 4, 1968), pp. 395 f.

————. "Effective Negativism" (letter to the editor), *The Mennonite* (Apr. 21, 1964), p. 272.

————. "Tax Refusal as Conscientious Objection to War," *Mennonite Quarterly Review*, Vol. XLIII, No. 3 (July 1969), pp. 234-246.

Schmidt, Steven G. "Telephone Tax Vigil" (letter to the editor), *The Mennonite* (May 4, 1971), p. 302.

Schmidt, Mrs. Wanda (Steven). "Sees No End to the War" (an open letter to the President of the U.S.), *The Mennonite* (Dec. 8, 1970), p. 760.

Scott, Lawrence. "Words Are Not Enough," *Liberation* (May 1957), pp. 14, 15.

Seguy, Jean. Book Review of *What Belongs to Caesar?* Archives De . . . . Des Religions.

Shelly, Andrew R. "Taxes for Military Spending," *The Mennonite* (July 18, 1961), p. 450, or the *Gospel Herald* (July 18, 1961), pp. 622 f.

————. "What About Taxes? *The Mennonite* (Sept. 13, 1960), p. 584.

Shelly, Maynard. "Can You Teach an Old Dog New Tricks?" — an editorial, *The Mennonite* (Jan. 29, 1963), p. 80.

————. "Mad Enough to Kill" (editorial), *The Mennonite* (June 15, 1971), p. 404.

————. "Western District Takes Stand on War Taxes," *The Mennonite* (Nov. 10, 1970), pp. 682-84.

Shoemaker, W. Warren. "Respect for the Laws of the Land," *Messenger* (June 18, 1970), pp. 9-11.

"Should We Pay Tax Which Goes for Militarism?" *The I-W Mirror* (Mar. 7, 1960), p. 2. (Responses to this question given in issues of Mar. 21 and Apr. 4.)

Smoker, Art. "Readers Say," *Gospel Herald* (July 18, 1972), p. 586.

Smucker, Don E. "Whither Christian Pacifism?" *Mennonite Quarterly Review*, Vol. 23, No. 4 (October 1949), pp. 257-68.

Snyder, Graydon F. "Obedience or Disobedience? An Understanding of Romans 13," *Messenger* (Church of the Brethren), Vol. 119, No. 3 (Jan. 29, 1970), pp. 8-10.

Souder, Eugene K. "Nonresistant People and the Federal Income Tax," *Gospel Herald* (Dec. 27, 1960), p. 1103, and the *Mennonite Quarterly Review* (Dec. 29, 1960), p. 6.

Sprunger, Barton T. "Most of All Foolish — II" — letter to Mr. Myers. *The Mennonite*, 83:23 (June 4, 1968), p. 395.

Stauffer, James K. "War Taxes Questioned," *Gospel Herald* (June 2, 1970), p. 505.

Steelberg, Donald R. "The Whole Body Acts" — a letter to the editor. *The Mennonite* (Nov. 22, 1966), p. 716.

Stendahl, Krister. "Hate, Non-Retaliation, and Love and Romans 12:19-21," *Harvard Theological Review*, Vol. 55, No. 4 (October 1962), pp. 343-55.

Stoltzfus, Victor. "What About Taxes for War Purposes?" *Christian Living* (July 1961), pp. 38, 39.

Stone, Mardy Rich. "Support for Tax Refusers" (letter to the editor), *The Mennonite* (June 5, 1962), p. 380.

Suderman, Elmer F. "The Comfortable Pew and the Tangled World," *Mennonite Life* (January 1967), pp. 3, 4.

Swarr, John. "Readers Say," *Gospel Herald* (Aug. 1, 1972), p. 618.

Swarr, John S. "New Christian Life-Style" (letter to the editor), *The Mennonite* (Feb. 2, 1971), p. 77.

"Taxes and War," *Between the Lines* (May 1, 1970), p. 4.

"Thoreau, A Centenary Gathering," *The Massachusetts Review*, University of Massachusetts, Amherst, Mass. (an issue of 1963, apparently).

"Tolstoy's Writings on Civil Disobedience and Non-Violence," *Fellowship* (November 1967), p. 32.

Uphaus, Willard. "Conscience and Disobedience," *The Massachusetts Review* (Autumn, 1962).

Vogt, Virgil (ed.). "Radical Reformation Reader," *Concern No. 18* (a pamphlet series for questions of Christian renewal), July 1971.

Von Selle, Margaret. "On Praying for Peace and Paying for War," *The Peacemaker* (Apr. 9, 1960), pp. 2 and 4.

"War Tax Concern," *The Mennonite* (July 28, 1959), p. 461.

War tax information request in *Christian Living* (May 1969) Box 569, Scottdale, Pa. 15683, p. 39.

"War Tax Refusal" (including book review of *What Belongs to Caesar?*), *The Post-American, Voice of the People's Christian Coalition* (Summer, 1972), Vol. 1, No. 4.

Weaver, Amos W. "Our Readers Say — ," *Gospel Herald* (Apr. 2, 1963), p. 268.

Weir, T. H. "Luke XX, 20," *Expository Times*, Vol. 28 (June 1917), p. 426.

"Western District Discusses Tax Refusal, Automated War," *The Mennonite* (Mar. 21, 1972), p. 205.

"Western, Eastern Meetings to Discuss War Tax Payment," *The Mennonite* (Feb. 22, 1972), p. 135.

Westing, Arthur H., and E. W. Pfeiffer. "The Cratering of Indochina," *Scientific American* (May 1972), pp. 20-29.

White, Terence Gervais. "Render Unto Caesar," *Hibbert Journal*, Vol. 44, No. 174 (April 1946), pp. 263-70.

Wilson, Edmund. "The Cold War and the Income Tax," *Liberation* (December 1963), p. 25.

Wingell, Bill. "The Connection," *Liberation* (December 1963), p. 28.

Wofford, Harris. "The Law and Civil Disobedience," *The Presbyterian Outlook* (Sept. 26, 1960), pp. 5, 6.

"Workshop Questions Morality of War Taxes," *The Mennonite* (Feb. 1, 1972), p. 75.

Yoder, Edward. "Christianity and the State," *Mennonite Quarterly Review*, Vol. XI, No. 3 (July 1937), pp. 171-195.

—————. "The Obligation of the Christian to the State and Community — 'Render to Caesar,'" *Mennonite Quarterly Review*, Vol. XIII, No. 2 (April 1939), pp. 104-122.

Yoder, John Howard. "The Anabaptist Dissent: The Logic of the Place of the Disciple in Society," *Concern*, No. 1 (June 1954), pp. 45-68.

—————. "The Otherness of the Church," *Mennonite Quarterly Review*, Vol. XXXV, No. 4 (October 1961), pp. 286-96.

—————. "The Things That Are Caesar's," Parts I, II, & III, *Christian Living* (July 1960), pp. 4, 5, 34; (August 1960), pp. 14-17, 39; (September 1960), pp. 16-18.

—————. "Why I Don't Pay All My Income Tax" (a personal testimony), *Gospel Herald* (Jan. 22, 1963), pp. 81 and 92, and/or *The Mennonite* (Feb. 26, 1963), pp. 132-34.

Young, William Henry. "Why I Am Not a Tax Refuser," *The Christian Century* (May 16, 1962), pp. 625 f.

Zahn, Franklin. "Tax Refuser's Side" (letter to the editor), *The Christian Century* (June 27, 1962), p. 816.

—————. "They Can Afford It," *Fellowship* (April 1957), p. 13.

—————. "Christians and Caesar's Taxes," *The Christian Century* (Nov. 11, 1970), pp. 1349-52.

Zahn, Gordon. "The Religious Basis of Dissent," *Mennonite Quarterly Review*, Vol. XLII, No. 2, (April 1968), pp. 132-143.

INDEXES

Index of Scriptural References

Old Testament

Genesis 14:20 18
Genesis 32:13-21 18
Exodus 9:29 65
Exodus 19:5 65
Exodus 30:11-16 24
Joshua 16:10 18
Joshua 17:13 18
Judges 1:28-35 18
I Samuel 8:10-18 18
I Samuel 13:1f. 18
2 Samuel 24 19
1 Kings 4:7ff. 18, 19
1 Kings 5:13 18
1 Kings 10:14-29 19
1 Kings 10:15 19
1 Kings 12:1ff. 19
1 Kings 12:4 19
1 Kings 20:3 66
2 Kings 15:20 19
2 Kings 16:8 18
2 Kings 17:4 18
2 Kings 18:35 19
2 Kings 23:35 20
1 Chronicles 22:2 18
1 Chronicles 29:11-16 65
2 Chronicles 2 18
2 Chronicles 17:5 19
2 Chronicles 32:23 19
Ezra 4:13 20
Nehemiah 10:32-34 24
Psalm 24:1 . . . . 65, 97
Psalm 89:11 65
Psalm 104:24 65
Proverbs 24:21 55
Isaiah 2 73
Isaiah 27:11b 9
Isaiah 31:1f. 62
Isaiah 45:5, 6, 18b, 22 28
Isaiah 46:9 28

Jeremiah 43:10a 49
Micah 4 73
Haggai 2:8 65

Intertestamental Literature

2 Maccabees 3:1 — 4:6 21
Jos. Antiq. 19:6; 3 24

New Testament

Matthew 5 73
Matthew 17:24-27 . . 24, 32-35, 37
Matthew 22:15-22 . . . . 32, 35, 52
Matthew 22:17 24
Mark 12:13-17 . . . . . 32, 35-42, 65
Mark 12:44 33
Luke 2:1-7 24
Luke 5:30 21
Luke 20:20-26 . . . . 32, 35
Luke 23:2 37
Acts 3:1 34
Acts 4, 5 56
Acts 5:29 . . . . 32, 56, 58
Acts 5:36, 37 . . . . 25, 56
Romans 12, 13 . . . . . . 43ff., 73
Romans 13:1-7 . . . . 32, 42-54, 55
Romans 14:1 — 15:13 43
1 Corinthians 1:27a 96
1 Corinthians 2:8 45
1 Corinthians 4:10a 95
1 Corinthians 6:1f. 32
Galatians 5 48
Ephesians 5:33 55
Ephesians 6:12 53
Philippians 3:10 94
1 Timothy 1:19 94
1 Timothy 2:1f. 32
1 Timothy 5 73
1 Peter 2:13-17 . . . . 32, 52, 54-56
Revelation 13 . . . . 52, 56
Revelation 19 56

Index of Names and Subjects

Aesculapian oath, 62
Algonquin Indians, 74
American Revolution, 75, 76
Amish, 62
Anabaptists, 29, 71ff., 83, 94-95
anarchists, 71
Antipater (*see* Herod the Idumaean)
apathy, 87
Aukerman, Dale, 81
Baez, Joan, 81
baptism, believer's, 94
Barabbas, 38
Ben-hadad, King, 66
biblical interpretation, 45, 56, 72
Bill of Rights, 29
Bonhoeffer, Dietrich, 89
Borsodi, Ralph, 59
Brockington, L. H., 39
Bromley, Ernest R., 37, 40, 83
Bull, Wendal, 93
Caesar, 22, 24, 27, 28, 31, 35, 38,
   46, 48, 55, 56, 65, 74, 86, 88, 91,
   92, 97
church and state, 47, 52, 53, 84, 85,
   86, 94 (separation of)
Church of the Brethren, 81, 82-83
Churchman, John, 75
citizenship, 56, 60, 61, 91
civil disobedience, 42, 50, 51, 59,
   60, 62, 79, 80, 83, 93, 95
conscience, 47, 50, 51, 56, 58, 59,
   60, 70, 71, 73, 74, 75, 78, 79,
   81, 83, 85, 93, 94, 96
conscription (of men or money), 66,
   77, 81, 82, 85, 90, 97
Cranfield, C. E. B., 43-44, 51, 55
Cullmann, Oscar, 37f., 45f., 53-54
Daniel, 38
David, King, 19
De Boer, Hans A., 64
Deak, Francis, 78
Derrett, J. Duncan M., 33-34
discipleship, 12, 95
Dunkards, 76-77
Eisenhower, Dwight D., 68-69
Enz, Jacob J., 43
Epp, Frank H., 92

eschatology, 51
ethics, 44, 47, 51, 60-64, 69, 71, 82,
   91, 96 (versus the collective will)
Fast, Henry, 41
Ferdinand, King, 72
Fort Amsterdam, 74
Franklin, Benjamin, 31
Franz, John, 66-67
freedom, religious, 58-59, 73, 77, 85,
   90, 94
Friesen, J. John, 95
Funk, Christian, 77
Gale, Herbert M., 48-49
Gandhi, Mahatma, 79-80
government, 27, 31, 41, 42ff., 51, 54
   (purpose of), 55, 56, 58, 63, 65,
   67, 72, 79
Grant, Frederick C., 26-7, 37ff.
Gregg, Richard B., 78
Hackman, Walton N., 8
Harvey, Arthur, 36
Hassler, Alfred, 59
Heliodorus, 21
heresy, 45
Herod the Great, 22f.
Herod the Idumaean, 22
Herodians, 35
Herodotus, 20
Hezekiah, 19
Hubmaier, Balthasar, 72-73
Hut, Hans, 72
Hutterites, 72, 73
Hyrcanus, high priest, 22, 26
Hyrcanus, "son of Tobias," 21
idolatry, 27, 36, 46-48, 71, 87, 88,
   90
individual versus state, 11f., 63, 83
   84, 88, 89-90, 91, 94, 96, 97
Internal Revenue Service, 30, 57,
   66, 81, 82, 83, 87, 91, 92, 93
Iroquois Indians, 74
Israel, 20
Janzen, Lester E., 66
Jehoiakim, King, 20
Jehoshaphat, 19
Jeremiah, 88-89
Jeroboam, 19

Jesus Christ, 33ff., 47, 54, 61, 64, 65, 87, 88 (as Lord), 91, 94, 95 (death on the cross), 96-97
Jewish war of AD 70, 28
Jones, Rufus M., 76
Josef, Franz, 78
Joseph and Mary, 24
Joseph ben Tobiah, 21
Josephus, 20, 24, 25, 65
Judah, 20, 88
Judas of Galilee, 25, 27, 28
Judas Maccabaeus, 38
Juhnke, James C., 67
Kaunitz, Four brothers of, 73
Kennard, J. Spencer, Jr., 38f., 65, 67
Kieft, William, 74
King, Dwight Y., 60, 83, 89
King, Martin Luther, Jr., 79
kingship, divine, 27, 40, 48, 55, 58-60, 64, 65, 86, 88
kingship, human, 19, 27, 48, 55, 60, 63, 88
Klausner, J., 39
König, Eduard, 20
Lasserre, Jean, 41, 42, 52, 71
Law, 48f.
Leenhardt, F. J., 52
Liechtenstein, Lord, 73
Littell, Franklin Hamlin, 72
Love, 13, 42ff., 48, 54, 60-64, 81, 86, 89, 91, 96-97
Lowell, James Russell, 63, 67
Lynd, Staughton, 76
McCrackin, Maurice, 83, 96-97
Maccabaeus, Judas (*see* Judas Maccabaeus)
Macdonald, Dwight, 89-90
Macgregor, G. H. C., 41
Magna Charta, 29
martyrs, 55
Mayer, Milton, 62
Mayer, Peter, 76
Meinhold, Peter, 44, 50
Mennonite Biblical Seminary, 7
Mennonites, 29, 59, 62, 68, 71ff., 81, 83, 84 (French), 88, 92
Messiah, 40
Metzler, Edgar, 92
Michel, O., 43
militarism, 12, 62, 67, 69f., 90, 93, 97

"military-industrial complex," 69
Montefiore, Hugh, 33, 34
Morrison, Clinton D., 44, 50-51
Muste, A. J., 80-81, 83, 93
Nebuchadnezzar, 49
Nerva, 25
Nikolsburg disputation of 1527, 72-73
nonresistance, 76, 77
nonviolent resistance, 91
Nürnberg War Crimes Trials, 90
Osborne, Governor, 59-60
Parkinson, C. Northcote, 31, 70
Paul, Apostle, 45, 46, 47, 48, 49, 50, 52, 53, 54, 55, 56, 71, 96
Peacemaker Movement, 82
Pearson, Roy, 68
Penn, William, 74
Pentagon, 64, 87
persecution, 53, 54, 56, 73
Peter, Apostle, 54-56, 58
Pharaoh Neco, 20
Pharisees, 33ff.
Pilate, 28, 40
Polish Brethren, 74
prison, 55, 79
"publicans," 21
Quakers, 73, 74ff., 82
reconciliation, 63, 64
Rehoboam, 19
Reimer, Klaas, 76
Revolution, French, 29
Riedemann, Peter, 73
Rist, Martin, 54
Rome, the Romans, 21, 23, 25, 28, 46, 49, 56
Rudolph II, Emperor, 73
Rutenber, Culbert G., 41
Sadducees, 33ff.
Samuel, 18
Sanders, J. A., 19
Sartin, Nancy E., 31
Saul, King, 49
sin, 68, 88, 94
Slaubaugh, Daniel, 88
Solomon, 18f., 23
Stauffer, Ethelbert, 28, 41
Steen, John E., 63
stewardship, 64-70, 82
suffering, 51, 54, 61, 67, 69, 75, 78,

84, 86, 90, 94-95
Sweet, William Warren, 7
Swiss Brethren, 72
Synge, John, 11
tax, half-shekel, 24, 32f.
tax, income, 20f., 30f., 57, 62, 66
  68, 81, 82, 93
tax on telephone service, 57
Tax, Temple, 32ff.
Taxation, Compulsory, 18, 19, 57,
  81, 85
Taxation, History of, 17ff., 57, 62,
  71-85, 96
Taxation, Withholding system of,
  30, 82, 84-85
temple in Jerusalem, 23, 25, 34, 40
temple of Jupiter Capitolinus in
  Rome, 25, 34, 40-41, 71
Theudas, 25
Thomas, Norman M., 59
Thoreau, Henry David, 78-79
Tolstoy, Leo, 79
tribute, 19ff., 25, 26, 27, 34, 39f.,
  53, 66, 74
tyranny, 31

United Nations, 68, 82 (UNICEF)
United States of America, 30, 31,
  57, 68, 69, 79, 87, 91
Ventidius, 28
Vespasian, 25
Vietnam, 69, 95 (crisis)
war, 28, 61, 62, 63, 64, 66, 69f.
  (and waste), 94
War, Civil, 30, 77
War, French and Indian, 75
war, god of, 90
Wars, Napoleonic, 30, 76
Webster, Ted, 87
Weinberg, Arthur and Lila, 76
Wells, Charles A., 69-70
Woolman, John, 74-75
worship, emperor, 27, 46f., 52, 55,
  58
Yeats, William Butler, 11
Yoder, John Howard, 49-50, 51-52,
  84, 93-94
Zahn, Gordon, 91
Zealots, 27, 36, 38
Zehr, Daniel, 67-68

Donald D. Kaufman of Newton, Kansas, is employed as an applicator for an insulation business. Born on a farm near Marion, South Dakota, in 1933, he has served in the capacities of MCC field director, pastor, and as personnel coordinator.

He holds the MDiv degree from Associated Mennonite Biblical Seminaries, a BDiv degree from Mennonite Biblical Seminary, a BA from Bethel College, North Newton, Kansas, and an AA from Freeman Junior College, Freeman, South Dakota.

Kaufman's writing has appeared in *Sojourners, The Mennonite, Gospel Herald,* and *Pulpit Digest.* He has prepared study papers on the war tax issue as a conscientious objector to war and is author of *The Tax Dilemma: Praying for Peace, Paying for War* (Herald Press, 1978).

Donald and Eleanor (Wismer) Kaufman are members of the Bethel College Mennonite Church. They are the parents of Kendra Janean, Galen David, and Nathan Dean.